James A. Greene
3/21/26.

Spanish Bayonet

STEPHEN VINCENT BENÉT

Spanish Bayonet

by
Stephen Vincent Benét

NEW YORK
GEORGE H. DORAN COMPANY

Contents

The Barbary Ape

SPANISH BAYONET

PRELUDE:

The Barbary Ape

THEY were dancing in the streets of Port Mahon.

The time was shortly after Easter in the year of our Lord, 1769. Christ had died and risen again in the Cathedral, with flowers and candleflame and the songs of Easter Eve, when strollers pass through the narrow, rocky streets, singing the Fromajardis— the sorrows of Mary—and receive through opened lattice and shutter, small sanctified gifts of sweet-meats and pastry from hands blurred by the dusk. This year the sweetmeats had been few and poor, for the scanty crops of Minorca had failed for the third successive season, and all Lent the Vicar-General had excused his afflicted children from their duty of abstinence, so pinched were the times. But now, with the resurrection of the earth and the grave twilights of April, there was hope in the air, and the tiled and terrace-roofed houses that clung together in a town against the rock, like the nests of swallows upon a chimney of stone, knew again the music of the guitar.

Below, in the famous harbor where all the fleets of Europe might ride at anchor, lay the ships which had brought that hope. Minorca had too many children to feed from a narrow and indurate breast— the ships would take some away, over the ocean, to a new country, where the British flag flew from the top of a palm-tree in the Floridas of America, and, after four years of labor for the master of the expedition, a man might claim his own fifty acres of fertile ground and take his siesta at noon in the shadow of his own trees.

Sebastian Zafortezas, looking down at the harbor through the clear darkness, made out the riding-lights of those ships, and pondered the strange benevolencies of the English. Quick, loud-voiced, red-faced men who swore without punctilio and prayed without courtesy, who bathed themselves unnecessarily in frigid waters as a preparation for future torments of incessant fire, they nevertheless displayed an extraordinary unwillingness to let newly-reconquered subjects die quietly of starvation. They were all a little mad, of course, and the master of the ships in the harbor no doubt as mad as any.

A doctor they called him, but Sebastian could hardly believe it. He was not like Spanish doctors, seemly and mournful, as befits one who immediately precedes the priest and the undertaker, but spry and perpetually smiling with clean hands and a gentleman's wig. Moreover the English governor had received him with much honor, which even an English governor would hardly show to one whose avouched occupation was not much better than that of a burier-beetle. Ah well, it was all one, thought Sebastian—doctor or prince, he had given the word of an Englishman as to the rewards which might be gained by those who embarked with him as colonists for the distant country—and the word of an Englishman, no matter how mad, was good. Minorca had learned that in her last fifty years of shuttlecocking between the Powers—and the hearts of her people cherished few romantic yearnings for reunion with Spain.

Spain was well enough, but they were the people of the islands. They had given sailors to Carthage and slingers to Rome, their rocks held deserted altars to gods forgotten before the Cross. Their pilots had known the sea when Prince Henry the Navigator was a royal doll in swaddling-clothes, and it was said of them on the mainland that the poorest fisherman of the islands was prouder than three grandees.

As Sebastian gazed at the harbor, he felt a wave of unexpected sickness strike at his heart at the thought of never seeing it again nor any of the streamless island of doves and eagles, but it soon passed. At the age of fifteen he was admittedly a man and men did not suffer from homesickness. Besides, there was nothing else to do. His uncle could not keep him in Port Mahon any longer; there were

enough mouths in that house already. And the hut
near the Altar of the Gentiles, in the boulders of
Fererias, where he had been born and lived till a
year ago, had been picked clean before his mother
died. He had her rosary of sea-snail shells and his
father's knife; that was all one could expect.

Moreover, his adventure would not be a lonely
one. When the ships passed out by St. Philip's
Castle next week, on the track the beaten Almojarife
had travelled toward Barbary with his people, his
books of magic, his Moorish gowns and his fifty
swords, more than a thousand Mahonese would be
aboard, men, women and children, pet lizards, pots
and scapulars. Sebastian saw himself in the future
for an instant, gazing out over the foreign landscape
of his fifty acres with a burst ripe fig half-eaten in
his hand and a child making scrawls with a stick in
the dust before his doorstep. Then he turned away
from his post of musing with a smile on his mouth.

He had made his confession at Easter and been
absolved—the past was balanced, the future incom-
prehensible,—but tonight he could dance with a free
heart. He followed the clue of the music along
mazy alleyways, his body a little giddy at times
from weeks of undernourishment, but his mind at
peace. At last he came out where the wider street
was crowded with the grave dancers and the throb
of the guitars echoed like silver blood in the dark

veins of heaven. He stood for a moment, observing the scene.

The street was lit by torches—occasionally one of them would sputter and send up a shower of tiny golden bees in the still air. Beneath them the dissolving patterns of the dance formed and broke and reformed again like a shower of the colored petals of flowers stirred by light wind. The women danced discreetly, their eyes cast on the ground; the men were more extravagant in their gestures; but in the faces of both, the eyes were large with starvation and solemn with joy. The rebozillas pinned about the heads of the women did not hide the faint hollows in their cheeks—hunger had given them a new and extenuate beauty—their feet seemed lighter to them and a little mad. The red worsted girdles of the men were drawn tighter about their bodies, their cheeks showed the play of hunger too, but their broad flat shoes of white leather slapped gallantly on the stones; and in a corner of shadows the musicians plucked at their ribboned instruments yet more swiftly and the dance went on and on, without beginning or end.

Occasionally, without apparent reason, the musicians would give in unison a short sonorous cry, and the bystanders would call out at once "Long live the dancers!" in reticent approval, to be echoed by a low, soft murmur from the dancers of "Long live the lookers-on!" Such was the courtesy of Minorca, and to Sebastian, as he watched, the murmurous call and response turned to the perpetual cooing of the ringdoves in the sea-caves where his father had been drowned and the red of worsted girdle and Phrygian cap was the blood of the sun sinking into the waters of evening above the Altar of the Gentiles, and music touched at the heart, and an island was hard to leave. But presently he found himself dancing, too —aloofly and arrogantly as befits a man of fifteen.

He hardly noticed his partner—the torches threw confusing shadows, her eyes were averted, her mouth hidden behind her black fan. Presently one of the bystanders called out to him gayly in the permissible words, "Say a word to her! Say a word to her!" He responded mechanically in the set and ancient compliment, "What would you have me say to her but that she has the face of a rose?" and there was a clapping of hands. But her face, as the fan drooped aside for an instant in acknowledgment, was not like that of a rose but a darker and more barbarous flower. He sought idly for the name of such a flower for a moment, then the thought passed from his mind and the pattern of the dance took its place. "Ha! Ha!" cried the musicians and stamped their feet—"Spain! Spain!" twanged the strings of the guitars.

It was some time later and Sebastian was wholly absorbed in the flow of the dance, when the little ape on the roof of one of the houses overlooking the street, decided that there might be pickings down among men if he were bold enough to go and look for them. He was very hungry but equally terrified and the more recent events of his life had given him little confidence in humanity. Bought from a Barbary Jew by the master of a Spanish merchantman and sold again in Mahon harbor to a drunken private of the Royal Irish Foot, he had tasted the characteristics of three different nations of mankind in the last few weeks and found each as bitter and strange as the cold, stinging waters of the sea. He was a young, uninstructed ape, smaller than most of his tail-less species—and his disposition normally inclined toward the cheerful. But his heart was gloomy now, and the fur of his body miserable.

There were neither proper victuals nor people of his race in this stony region and he could not forget the fight between his latest master and another bellowing, red-furred giant which had given him his liberty some hours ago. The sergeant had made suggestions anent the succulent qualities of roasted monkey which the other had not treated with due respect—but a knowledge of this was spared the cause of the combat who regarded all the various, inexplicable noises emitted by the human race with the same timid disdain. Their occupations, too, seemed both futile and mysterious, he thought as he shivered on his rooftop, watching the dance. One never could expect anything of them but curious pawings and tweakings and a series of imprisonments in places that smelt indelicately of humanity. But his hunger drove him, and presently he slipped down the wall of the house to crouch a moment in the shadows at its foot, peering about with quick, startled, melancholy eyes.

The dancers did not observe him but a boy half-asleep in a doorway did, came awake abruptly and ran, shouting and waving his arms. Quite distraught with terror at once, the monkey lost his wits completely and darted blindly between the feet of the dancers. Great jostling bodies trampled all about him and his nostrils were full of the unpleasing odor of man. He ran this way and that confusedly for an instant while everyone shouted and pointed, and then suddenly leaped for refuge at something tall and stationary which, if Fate were really a monkey, might prove to be some new sort of tree. It was not a tree but a man, and he knew it while he was yet in the air, but at least he was off the dangerous ground. He clung to the man's shirt, half-dead and hardly daring to breathe. But the man stayed perfectly still, and, after a while, the monkey felt a finger rubbing his fur the right way.

The incident had only halted the dance for a moment. It continued now; the boy, his brief excitement forgotten, fell asleep in his doorway again; "Say a word to her! Say a word to her!" called the loungers by the walls to another dancer; the music caught new fire from crafty hands. Sebastian was the only person much affected—he had dropped out of the dance and stood a little removed now, gently stroking the monkey's back.

He could not have said why he had protected the little creature—the Latin has no great native tenderness for animals, and while monkeys were a rarity in Minorca, no one but a mad Englishman would buy such a thing. But as he looked into the wrinkled and mournful face of the animal clinging at his breast, he knew that he intended to keep it if he could, even take it with him on his travels. It was bad to refuse shelter to the shelterless, and, though this petitioner had no soul, he came dressed as a friar and so deserved the hospitality of a Christian—but those were not the real reasons, "Besides, we are both alone in the world," thought Sebastian—but that was no reason, either, for a world where many were alone. What the true springs of his action had been, he could not have said.

"You shall have a little gold collar and sit on a perch when I have my fifty acres" he confided to the monkey. The monkey, hearing a new noise, thought he was to be beaten and looked up prepared to bite—so it seemed to Sebastian as if he had understood. After a moment Sebastian fumbled a piece of cord from his pocket and tied one end about the monkey's neck—an attention the latter accepted with passive resignation—at least this latest owner seemed quieter than the others. "There," said Sebastian, "No, you must not bite at the cord—we are going to the Floridas, monkey, you and I—we shall be rich there, monkey," and he pulled his coat around further so the monkey should be warm. Then his eyes turned away from his new possession and lost themselves in watching the dance—and presently the girl who had been his partner and whose face was like some flower more savage than the rose came over and stood near him, her fan moving in a slow regular beat that ruffled the soft black fur on the top of the monkey's head.

PART ONE: *The Pride of the Colonies*

PART ONE:

The Pride of the Colonies

Some five years later, the merchantman, "Pride of
the Colonies," bound out of New York for St.
Augustine, was running before a fresh breeze down
the blue, sparkling plain of the Atlantic. The single
passenger she carried, a young man named Andrew
Beard, was seated in a sort of improvised chair by
the lee-rail, watching the milk-streaked ribbon of
her wake dwindle out continually along the broad,
endless back of the sea, with that idle, rather
pleasant monotony of mind which comes to those
who have been many days on the water without
much active occupation. A small, brown, dumpy
copy of Mr. Pope's translation of the Iliad lay in his
lap, and his forefinger mechanically kept the place
where he had left off reading. He had been drawn
from the book by a certain, inert curiosity as to
whether the color of the waters of any ocean might
fitly be compared with the color of wine—and hav-
ing decided, sleepily, that not even the palest vin-
tages of the Rhine, beheld through green Venetian
glass, could match the occasional streaks of lucid
emerald where the trace of the ship's wake grew

faint as the imprint of a feather on velvet, had excused himself from further concern at present with the doings of the well-greaved Achæans.

He had never felt either so well or so lazy and New York and the life he had led till this voyage began seemed very small and distant—a diminutive red city with paper snow on its gables, imprisoned in a glass bubble that the sea had washed away. To-morrow, Captain Stout had said, they were likely to sight the lighthouse on Anastasia Island, and journey's end—but at the moment the journey still seemed infinite. It was impossible to think that in a little while the last sound in his head as he fell asleep at night would not be the strain of the breeze in the cordage and the complaint of wood against wind and water or that he would ever rise again in the morning to look out upon a solid and unfluctuating world. Nevertheless, these things would be so, and swiftly. It behooved him, against his will, to think of what lay in store for him beyond the horizon, and why he had lived all this time with a seashell held close to his ear.

A series of inconsecutive pictures passed before his eyes. He was a little boy, stiffly seated in a high, banister-backed chair before a gleaming mirror, his eyes sober with excitement, as that most impressive of men, his father's barber, who lived in a shop full of sweet-smelling bottles with a great gold basin hung over the front door, arranged upon his shorn head with deft, pale, long fingers the tiny, marvellous wig that had come in a box from London, and, wonder of wonders, crowned it at last with a little laced hat, just like his older brother's even to its Kevenhuller cock.

He smiled—how proud he had been of that ridiculous wig and what a fight he had had with the butcher's boy who had asked him jeeringly if old Sandy Beard was setting up for a Lord. Fashions had changed, and little boys could wear their own hair now, even when their fathers were as important merchants as Alexander Beard. The thought called up an image of his father's huge, cool storehouses down by the water and a gang of negroes, singing together in rich, deep, mournful voices, as they unloaded merchandise consigned to Alexander Beard and Son from a ship just come to port from strangely-painted corners of the map. Wherever the commerce of New York Colony voyaged, Alexander Beard's name was known and his signature good.

The storehouses disappeared, and in their place, for some reason, Andrew saw the silver-sanded floor of a Dutch kitchen. He was munching an oelykoek and Gerrit Jans was telling him stolidly of the wonders of St. Nicholas who stuffed the wooden shoes of godly little boys in Holland with crullers and toy windmills and silver skates on his name-day. . . . The heavy, flowery scent of the catalpa-trees outside the King's Arms, on Broadway between Crown

and Little Prince Streets, where the officers came
from Fort George, mixed, somehow, with the odor
of mignonette and sweet-william in his mother's
garden in the country. She was walking along the
bricked path on a hot, Spring morning, with her
green calash shading her stern, fine face, and a small
painted basket of seeds in her hand.

Then he was one of a group of boys running home
past the Fort on a chill, green winter evening, not
daring to look aside lest Governor Sir Danvers
Osborne, who had hanged himself on the palisade
after five days of office, should suddenly be dangling
there to appal them, with his silk-handkerchief
noosed around his neck . . . he was sitting on his
brother Lucius's knees watching the historic cock-
fight out on the Germantown road when Massa-
chusetts Boy had beaten and killed Mr. Signet's long-
undefeated Cock of the North . . . he was walking
with his father underneath the arches of the Ex-
change, unspeakably proud at being allowed to hold
his father's gold-headed cane and see him converse
with the great ones of the city.

The images faded. He sighed, lazily. Boyhood
had been a good time. If he had never been as
dashing as Lucius, he had always admired Lucius
far too much to envy him and had been well con-
tent to take second place. As for Peggy, poor child,
he certainly did not envy her—with her stiff, buck-
ram stays clamped on her round, adolescent body,

and the long needle stuck upright in the front of her
dress for an hour each day to teach her to hold her
chin erect as a young girl of quality should. Some-
where among his baggage he had the letter case
stitched with red and green silk that had been her
damp, parting gift to him—and how she had begged
him to bring her home a little alligator from the
Floridas! He smiled amusedly. He felt quite old
enough to be Peggy's grandfather, now that he was
travelling alone on important business for his father
—though he was only twenty-one and she was four-
teen.

By the way, he must look at his new case of pistols
again. He had been warned particularly against
letting the sea-air rust them. But the thought of the
pistols brought up the troubled state of the times to
his mind, and his eyes narrowed. It seemed to him
that through all the years of his boyhood, New York
had been in a constant turmoil of celebrations and
protests and placards on the walls. The Stamp Act
—the Liberty poles—the repeal of the Stamp Act
and the new gilded statue of a togaed King George
ramping upon a fat, embarrassed charger in the
Bowling Green—the liberty boys with their rowdy
songs and their continual scuffles with the soldiers—
this tea business, now. Lucius, too—he knew that
his father suspected Lucius, for all his dandyism, of
secret affiliations with the more fashionable wing of
the so-called Friends of Liberty—young Gouver-

neur Morris and some of the Livingston set. He himself did not care so much for young Gouverneur Morris. His celebrated King's College oration upon Wit and Beauty might be of as marbled an elegance as the conversation of Rasselas, Prince of Abyssinia —but he wore a conscious little air of prodigy that irked Andrew's soul.

Andrew stirred, uneasily, and wondered what the latest news was from the madmen in Boston. He remembered his father's bitter description of that troublesome John Hancock—"a rattle-tongued spendthrift who has wasted two fortunes on fine clothes and sedition"—mincing along the streets at noonday in a scarlet velvet cap, red morocco slippers and a blue damask gown. It would have been fun, if you had been unlucky enough to be born in Boston, to paint yourself up like an Indian and dump tea chests into grey water. But it was a boy's exploit, for all that, hardly worth the attention of a level-headed New Yorker. When the New York tea-ship arrived, the world would see how a really civilized colony dealt with such matters. He was sorry to be out of it all—the meeting of protest at the City Hall had been most impressive, though noisy. Still, it was quite unthinkable that the present tangle would lead to anything really serious. They would repeal the tea-tax as they had repealed the Stamp Act—such pushing Massachusetts gentry as Hancock and Sam Adams would be taught a lesson—the Livingston faction sing smaller for a while—and people drive out in Italian chaises to Turtle Bay for fish-suppers to the end of time.

He yawned, and turning his head, took in the steady eyes and the broad, leathery chest of the helmsman of the ship. For a boyish moment he envied the man completely the easy strength of his hands, and the blue tail of the tattooed mermaid disappearing under his shirt. Then he told himself sternly that he had pistols in his cabin, and at twenty-one, was already the master of an errand that could command the bodies of a dozen such able seamen. He tried over a phrase or two of textbook Spanish in his mind and then, sailor and errand alike dismissed for the moment, settled back to reading Mr. Pope's Homer at the passage where Hector bids Andromache farewell in the choicest of Addisonian English.

2.

Nevertheless, in the privacy of his cabin that night, as he lay on one arm, staring out through the open porthole at stars that seemed already tropical and soft in a languid heaven, certain fragments of his last long conversation with his father recurred to his mind to trouble it obscurely. For one thing, not one of the many excellent reasons for his present journey to the South had seemed particularly urgent till the trouble over the tea-tax grew to a head.

He had suffered from colds and occasional fever for some two winters, and the doctor had diagnosed a weakness of the lungs and recommended a sea-voyage toward warmer climates—that was true enough. And it was undoubtedly true that, since his health had not permitted him to finish his course of studies at King's College, he should begin to learn the ins and outs of the great merchant-house of Alexander Beard and Son. But there had been something in his father's eyes, when they talked together of the trip, that had disquieted him. For one thing he had never conceived before that his father might be uncertain of or puzzled by anything on earth.

He had started out firmly enough with, "Andrew—how's your cough?"

"About the same, sir," said Andrew, coughing.

"H'm—sit down, lad—I thought so. Well, my son, you'll be rid of it shortly, if Dr. Summerall knows his business. Can you sail on the "Pride of the Colonies" for St. Augustine two weeks from now—on my business?"

"Yes sir," said Andrew, at once dumbfounded and very flattered. It was the first time in his life that his father had treated him entirely as an equal.

"Good son," said Alexander Beard and played with the feathers of a goose-quill a moment. "It may be business of weight, Andrew. I would go myself if," he hesitated, "if times were more settled, d'ye see?—yes—I might go myself—but as things are—" He frowned and lost himself in staring at something dubious he seemed to see in the wood of the table. After a while, "You may think it strange I don't send your brother," he said.

Here was something that Andrew, in the innocence of his heart, had never even considered. The glittering Lucius seemed to him far too splendid an adornment of the house of Beard to be spared for any such errand. He said something of the sort.

"Your obleeged servant sir, I'm sure, but Lucius is a damned macaroni!" said Alexander Beard abruptly, then, as Andrew grew rigid with loyalty, "Sorry, boy—I lost my temper then—but your brother, Lucius—if you can inform me why your brother Lucius" (the goose-quill rapped on his knuckles) "makes such friends of the pack of ranting Mohocks that set up barber's poles to Liberty all over the town—"

"My brother, sir," said Andrew, stiffly, "has his own political opinions, but—"

"But, but, but," said his father impatiently, "Oh your brother's a damned fine fellow—but he'll marry that Livingston wench before he's done and set the De Lanceys against him for good and all—if he doesn't do worse and go to bed with some Boston madam who thinks Sam Adams is God Almighty because he talks like a codfish. A plague on them all, I say—a plague out of Egypt—" He threw the snapped goose-quill aside.

Andrew was silent—his father's tempers were
rare, but when they came, they had to run their
course. He tried not to hear what his father was
saying about the Livingstons and the De Lanceys.
His father's passionate reverence for James De
Lancey, the dead ex-Governor, had always irked
him queerly, and he had never been able to see the
great, stately family coach roll by behind its famous
white horses without a secret feeling of discontent.
He remembered the time it had drawn up before
their own door and the arrogant, courteous, languid
gentleman who was carried like a phial of holywater
inside it had descended to take a glass of Malaga
with an Alexander Beard whose hands and manner
were suddenly and definitely obsequious. That had
happened when Andrew was only a small boy, but
the imprint of it had remained in his mind. He had
not been sorry, a little later, to stand in the crowd
and watch the long black worm of the funeral pro-
cession wind slowly, with its gilt-escutcheoned
hearse, toward Trinity Church, while the minute
guns from Copsey Battery tolled out the fifty-seven
years of the dead man's life.

"A great gentleman," his father was saying. He
sighed. "And yet one that would drink his glass of
wine in my house and never once—" He checked
himself.

Andrew stirred rebelliously. "Father! But why

should not even a gentleman like Governor De Lancey take wine in our house?"

"Why not indeed?" said his father, and smiled. "Why not indeed?"

The words were gently-spoken, but at their implication, Andrew felt the steady world rock under his feet.

"But, Father, we—we've always been—gentle—haven't we?"

"Gentle enough, of a surety," said his father, with eyes averted. "Or why should my eldest son be able to carry a sword?"

"But—the Beards of Westmoreland, sir—" said Andrew, horrified. Somehow, he had always taken gentility for granted. Now, in a brief moment, the very fabric of pleasant existence grew infirm.

"Aye," said his father, quietly. "The Beards of Westmoreland. Of a truth no one can say that there are not Beards in Westmoreland," and he actually chuckled. For an instant Andrew was appalled to find himself almost hating him. In his mind, he had walked through the green, English park of that Westmoreland estate a thousand times—he had rubbed the brown dust away with his finger from the names of the tombs in the chapel that ran back before Elizabeth. And yet, now that he came to think of it, park and manor-house and chapel alike had all been built of the insubstantial stuff of his own imagination. His father had never told him one word about his people. Now, suspicion once awake, he could see those imaginary ancestors and their signs of honor, crumble slowly to ash before him—leaving only a shopkeeper's family, uneasy with new-got riches, their backs supple whenever a gentleman passed in the street—and he felt naked and ashamed.

Something of what he felt and thought must have been written in his face, for "Dinna hurt yourself so, laddie," said his father now, his speech slipped suddenly back to the burr of the countryman, "That's the benefit of a new country. A man starts more even. And your mother's folk are gentle—and—well—we can all say with right that we're gentle, now. But nevertheless—no, ye wouldn't understand—but when Governor De Lancey came to my house—"

He left the words in the air, seeing their uselessness. What he said was true. Andrew could not understand. He could not look back through the years and see what his father saw—the little boy in the rough fur cap and the blue-yarn stockings staring round-eyed from the door of the catchpenny shop to see the fine gentleman's coach whirl past in a glory of gilt and glass and trampling white horses—the lank, burningly-ambitious, young man with ink on his fingers who had found in James De Lancey a patron worthy of worship. The little boy and young man had come a long and hazardous way to the impressive new house on the right side of

Wall Street, with its fashionable cupola and the Turkey carpets on its floors—but the stages of that epic were hidden from Andrew, and father and son looked at each other across a barrier that would not fall.

"Well, sir," said his father at last, breaking the deep silence, "As to this matter of the Floridas—"

The ensuing conversation helped Andrew back on his feet again at the time, though, remembered, certain things rose in a cloud of silver bubbles to fret him. He had always known his father's business interests wide, but now, for the first time, he saw them unroll before him like a parti-colored map on the dark table, and it made him proud. Even down in that strange, hot, spicy peninsula so lately Spain's, his father's eyes saw the long rows of indigo, cut down in the moment of flowering, and counted the profit of traffic with swamp Indians, hidden like alligators in the marshes, and the yield of fields of sugar cane he had never seen in the flesh.

It appeared that his father had had some dealings already with this Scotch Dr. Hilary Gentian who had brought his mixed cargo of Minorcans, Greeks and Italians to colonize the hammock-lands below St. Augustine. "An ingenious man, sir, but pressed for money—and the men in London never understand that. They think a colony grows as easily as a thistle patch, once it's seeded—'tis more like an asparagus-bed—you can't expect returns for the first

few years." Yet there had been some returns al-
ready—the indigo alone had brought in three thou-
sand pounds during the last year. "Then there are
his sugar works—and the hemp and maize and
barilla. But they began with over two thousand
souls to feed and were much harassed by sickness, I
understand. You must be free with your glass, boy,
when you reach there—they say a free glass wards
off the fevers."

Andrew listened dazzled, seeing the strange land-
scape rise before him with its blue sea and its tufted
palms and its smell of alien blossoms. And yet the
deep-seated reason, if there were one, for his imme-
diate departure remained unexplained to him. Dr.
Gentian had been warned of his probable arrival—
that made Andrew blink a little—his father had
never really mentioned the project before. He was
to remain at New Sparta for a number of months at
least—half-guest, half-apprentice in the ways of
such a plantation, always his father's agent. "I
would have you write me most fully of all that
comes to your mind—particularly as to whether
such a venture as Dr. Gentian's might be profitably
copied by other gentlemen of sufficient fortune."

Now what had his father meant by that? Surely
he could not be thinking of transferring part of his
interests to the distant Floridas? But there was
more. "Also, sir, and most particularly, I would
have you note the temper of the colony toward

these scatterbrains your brother admires so greatly.
I have heard that of all the colonies the Floridas
alone feel no whistle-belly grievance against the
Crown. If that be so—and these Gadarene swine
that call themselves sons of Liberty start running
their path to the sea—"

"But, sir, you cannot really think that—"

"I do not know," said his father, sombrely, "I do
not know. God knows there's no reason—but there.
I only know where the De Lanceys will stand—if it
comes to more than speechifying. And their interest
is mine."

"But why must your interest go with any other
man's interest?" said Andrew, touchily—the sting
still in the old wound his father had reopened.

"Because it must, boy. The one sure loser in any
conflict is your neutral—and we're not patroons.
It's lucky the Patroon's a minor—they'll be out of it
whatever happens. They'd think me mad at the
Coffee House if I told them what's at the back of
my mind, but let a few years pass and—if your
mother could see it as plain as I do and were better
able to stomach the trials of a new venture—But 'tis
little use talking of that and things may better some-
how—You'll need a new fowling-piece and some
light sort of gear—they say the sun is hot, though
not deadly as it is in India—"

So the conversation had flickered out into a dis-
cussion of Andrew's wardrobe and the climate, leav-

ing him with a feeling of mingled insecurity and pride. The abrupt extinction of those long-cherished kinsfolk, the Beards of Westmoreland, rankled now and then, but he could feel no scornful challenge to the accepted dignity of the house of Beard in the air of the city; and a fowling-piece with silver mounts soon wiped out the freshness of the hurt. On the whole he was too anxious to acquit himself well and too awed by the vague magnitude of his responsibilities, to give excessive thought to the gentility of his lineage, or the lack of it.

It occurred to him more than once that his father might be sending him away on a pretext to keep him from mixing too intimately with those friends of Lucius' who met every Thursday to drink toasts of a porcupine saddle, a cobweb pair of breeches and a long gallop to all enemies of Liberty. But even if the queer constraint of Lucius' farewell seemed to bear this theory out—he could not really believe in it when he thought it over. And it was equally impossible to believe with reason that his father actually considered abandoning the house on Wall Street and the cavernous storehouses by the docks for a palmetto-hut by a white-shawled strip of sand just because a row of wigs in a vague House of Parliament over the water had decided to impose a duty on certain, small, black dried leaves. And yet—

The days of the voyage gave him time to follow many such speculations to no conclusion. Of only one thing could he be sure. The fabric of life had always seemed secure and definite before—now he felt it give under his feet like a floor of fresh pine-boughs and saw things begin to grow unfamiliar that had always been familiar as water and light.

He gave the problem up and began to wonder drowsily just what he would find at New Sparta, Dr. Gentian had a Greek wife and a pair of daughters—or was it a daughter? He saw a tall, high-breasted girl with the face of Nausicáa—then her features sharpened—feathers came on her arms—was she harpy or eagle?—He did not know, but there was a soft thunder of wings about him for an instant, that passed away into the rumble of a cart over the paving-stones, a cart bringing sweet water to the house from the Tea-Water Pump—a blacka-moor got out of it, dressed in his brother Lucius' best scarlet coat and was offering him a basket of indigo in the name of Liberty as he fell asleep.

3.

The rumble of the cart was in his ears again as he woke, but he translated it swiftly into accustomed sounds. Bare feet ran on the deck above him to the piping whine of the bosun's whistle—cries answered a bawling voice. He jumped out of his bunk and felt something knock at his heart. Through the round porthole, like a picture held in the circle of a spyglass, was the white stone thumb of a lighthouse and a crawling line of foam on a beach——then, across more water, the vivid green of unexpected pines and the solid bones of land. The land had been an indented, meaningless line to starboard before, vanishing and reappearing again like a casual, evanescent mark scrawled hastily on the surface of the universal sea——now it lay broad across the path in a continent, and the sea shrank back again from the illimitable and savage world into measurable blue water, fretting the sides of a cup of rock and sand. He dressed hastily, in a mounting excitement and ran up on deck.

"Have to anchor outside the bar, sir," said Captain Stout, "The Pride's a lady——she draws more'n eight feet of water, she does——Now if she was one of your nasty little French baggages, *which* she ain't——"

Andrew nodded sagely, paying little attention. Now the actual land lay so plump before them, he felt a vast, unreasonable impatience at the various petty motions that must be gone through before they could set foot on it. The air seemed to him to smell of oranges already and he stared through the captain's spyglass feverishly, as if doing so would transport him at once to the shore.

"That's the Fort," said the Captain, pointing, "Spanishy-looking affair, *I* call it——see the lobster-

back walking post?   Cathedral's over there—don't
know as you can make it out—"   He chuckled,
"Queer souls, Spaniards, and that's a fact," he con-
fided, "No spit and polish about them—no, sir.
Don't even have any Christian sort of a bellringer in
the church—just a lame old codger to rattle the
bells with a stick."

Andrew turned to him with a thousand questions
on his tongue.

"How soon before we—"

"Oh, they know we're here," said the Captain,
chuckling again.   "See that boat, Mr. Beard?
Shouldn't be surprised if Dr. Gentian was aboard
her."   His throat suddenly became a leather
trumpet.   *"Aye, Mister Mate?"* he roared.   He
turned away.

The black, struggling bug in the waves jumped
into a longboat as Andrew put the glass to his eye
again.   He could see the sweat start on the backs
of the eight negro rowers as their oars rose and fell in
thrashing dumb-show.   But the figure in the stern-
sheets was what held his gaze—if it could be Doctor
Gentian.

He had expected such a different personage.   A
Scotch army-surgeon turned planter suggested,
somehow, a tall, rawboned, iron-mouthed dragoon
in patched kilts and a palmetto hat.   This spruce,
erect little figure with the chin and eyes of Cæsar was
dressed in black superfine broadcloth, with Mechlin

ruffles at the throat and wrists. His wig was freshly powdered, his gold-laced hat cocked in the fine extreme of fashion—even Lucius, Andrew thought, might have been a little awed by the sombre perfection of his attire. Andrew suddenly realized the incongruity of his own apparel with a start. He had dressed hastily, in the clothes he had worn during most of the voyage. After one glance through the spyglass at his host, the glazed hat borrowed from a sailor on his own head, the loose shirt and wide breeches he had thought so aptly nautical, made him feel as if he had strolled into White's in London painted like a Seneca chief. He cast a wild glance around him, but it was too late. They were lowering the Jacob's ladder already. In a moment Dr. Gentian would be aboard.

"Ahoy, Pride of the Colonies!" came a sharp clear voice from the water. "Ahoy, Captain Stout!"

"Ahoy sir!" called the Captain, "Stand by the ladder for Dr. Gentian, you sons of sweeps, or by God I'll—We've a passenger aboard for ye, Doctor!"

The spruce little Cæsar in black broadcloth called back something that the wind blew away. Then he was coming up the Jacob's ladder as nimbly as a fly. Andrew shivered with annoyance and embarrassment. Why hadn't the Captain told him the Doctor was like this?

"Mr. Beard?" said the man whom Andrew had

visualized as a kilted dragoon. There was a fresh breeze blowing, but not a drop of spray seemed to have spotted his black silk stockings and he stepped across the spattered deck with the quick daintiness of a cat. "Your obliged, obedient servant, Mr. Beard." A ring winked on his outstretched hand.

"Nay, yours, sir," said Andrew, diffidently, and stood staring.

He liked Dr. Gentian at first sight—there was something very merry about his mouth. Moreover, he had obviously taken in Andrew's strange attire at one rapid glance, and yet the sight had not perceptibly increased his merriment.

Captain Stout came bumbling up in a sort of respectful fury.

"Servant, Doctor Gentian—so you've met your passenger?—good, sir. You'll find him a bit broadened out since he started to voyage with us— none of your night-sweats now, eh, Mr. Beard?— and if you could have seen him set to his victuals after the first natteral squeamishness, sir—By God, the first day out, I thought he'd puke the very anchor up—but after that—"

Andrew felt with abhorrence that his ears were reddening, but Dr. Gentian saved him.

"The sea plays odd tricks on the best of us," he said easily, "I have seen an Admiral of the Blue hold his head in his cabin and wish himself a turnip-patch back on land—the first day out." He turned to Andrew, "I am glad to hear our good captain is so excellent a victualler. Do you snuff, Mr. Beard?"

"Thank you, sir," said Andrew gratefully, his fingers fumbling at fine rappee in a gold-and-tortoise shell box. The little act somehow set himself and Dr. Gentian apart from the effusive Captain in a world where the immodest allusions of such captains to nausea and victuals were the permitted liberties of old family servants.

"A weakness of mine, I fear," sighed Dr. Gentian, after an elegantly-managed sneeze. Andrew's sneezes had been far less elegant but he noted gratefully that Dr. Gentian had not been critical. Now, though, he grew a little brisk.

"But we must have you ashore, Mr. Beard, as soon as may suit your convenience. Have you breakfasted?"

"Not yet," said Andrew, suddenly conscious that he wished to very much.

Dr. Gentian put his palms together softly. "Excellent. Then you must do me the honor of breakfasting with me at Judge Willo's—we must set out for New Sparta, tomorrow, I fear, but meanwhile it is only fit you should meet some of the gentry of the town. Perhaps Captain Stout would favor us, also—"

"Thankee, Doctor." Somehow the captain had deflated in the last few minutes and seemed awk-

wardly aware of it. "But I shan't get ashore much
before noon, you know—"

"You deprive us of a pleasure, I assure you." The
Doctor was smiling again, "Mr. Beard, I venture to
hope, will not be so harsh."

"Delighted—certainly—Doctor Gentian," stam-
mered Andrew confusedly, "but—my luggage—"

"I am sure our good captain can send what you
find most necessary with us—the heavier luggage
can follow later. I have already settled for the
services of a barber for you, in case you should need
him. A sea-voyage is always trying to one's razors.
If there is anything else—you have only to command
me—I have a little business to transact with the cap-
tain—but if you could be ready to go ashore with
your small baggage in half an hour—Your servant
till then, sir."

"Yours," said a slightly bewildered but flattered
Andrew, and stumbled down below to strip him-
self hastily of the glazed hat in which he had taken
such pride and to thank his stars that he had aban-
doned the transient idea of having the bosun tattoo
the Royal Arms of Great Britain in blue across
his chest.

4.

The evening air was light with the frail sweetness
of crepe-myrtle; a little wind stirred in the trees like

the ghost of a humming-bird. In Judge Willo's dining-room, the cloth had long been drawn and the branched silver candlesticks at either end of the table cast shadowy pools of light that seemed to sink into the grain of the dark mahogany. The wreck of the dessert lay scattered like the relics of a battle-field—a great china punchbowl of bombo had succeeded the St. Lucar wine and gentlemen were beginning to be flushed and loquacious. Andrew, seated between Judge Willo and Dr. Gentian in the post of honor, sipped slowly at the cool deceptive compound of grated nutmeg, sugared water and Antigua rum, and felt a great indefinite affection for all humanity in general and the Floridas in particular rise in his heart.

He was wearing his best India-muslin cravat, his hair was clubbed and powdered, he felt clean and gay and at ease. Already he loved this little, lazy city whose trees were hung with the golden balls of oranges and whose houses were built of a multitude of tiny seashells weathered into stone. He would be sorry to leave it in the morning—the projecting balconies of the old Spanish dwellings had printed their shape on his heart. Many times, in the dreams before dawn, in the cold hour, he would wander the narrow swept streets, for years unmarred by the track of any wheeled vehicle, where the Spanish ladies in the old time had walked in their satin ball-slippers, at evening, with a languid grace.

He finished his glass of bombo with an air of wise melancholy—life was like that. The glass was re-filled—he drank again, abstractedly, musing on the world. Life was like that, yes. Life was an orange-tree—an orange-tree in flower—and he was getting a little drunk.

Only two things marred his perfect content—his interview with the Governor and the fact that his best shoe-buckles had been slightly tarnished by the sea-air. The Governor was a petulant, worried person who had treated him like a boy. But Dr. Gentian had behaved to the man with freezing civility and apologized for him to Andrew later. "An honest gentleman, Mr. Beard, but alas, no friend of mine." "Then no friend of mine, sir, I'll warrant you!" Andrew had cried sagaciously and Dr. Gentian had thanked him gravely and explained. It appeared that the best of St. Augustine was with them in lacking the Governor's approval.

The candles were growing very bright. Judge Willo's voice in his ear besought him to tell the company again the ridiculous tale of Governor Tryon's escape in his shirt from his burning house and how only the heavy snow on the roofs of the city had saved New York from a general conflagration that winter. It was an effort to find the proper words, but when he did, he was well repaid, for all the gentlemen laughed like thunder and Dr. Gentian clapped him on the back and called him a very Harry

Fielding for choiceness of wit. Then he tried to repeat some verse of Phillis Wheatley's, the young negro poetess who had just made such a stir, but broke down in the middle and only saved himself by saying that he hoped they understood he had meant no disrespect to Governor Tryon by his story.

"Governor Tryon's worthy gentleman," he heard himself repeating "They called him the Black Wolf in the Carolinas—but he's for the King! And we're all for the King here, aren't we—and damnation to liberty-boys? Who isn't for the King here?" he asked uncertainly, but his query was drowned in a roar of applause as they all stood up and drank to the King. Andrew, drinking too, felt the tears come to his eyes at the thought of such splendid loyalty to the King. He tried to picture the King to himself—he felt he should—but the features kept getting more and more uncertain.

A second bowl of bombo succeeded the first and, some time later, Andrew found himself by a window, gazing out into the garden. His legs seemed subject to occasional, inexplicable wabblings, but the night air, cool on his forehead, was a great refreshment. He glanced back at the room—a stertorous huddle of scarlet on the floor must be that pleasant Major from the garrison, succumbed at last to bombo and the force of gravity—the gentleman in plum-colored velvet whose name he could not remember was asleep with his head in a bowl of nuts—Judge

Willo seemed to be making indefinite attempts at
song. Andrew felt a great pride that he was still
soberly on his feet.

"They say our moonlight here is brighter than
yours in the North," said the serene voice of Dr.
Gentian in his ear.

" 'Tis very bright, in all conscience," said Andrew
a little thickly. The Doctor's glass had been filled
as often as any, but he seemed as yet quite untouched
by the revel. The small, demure, merry mouth was
composed and peaceful, the calm face showed only a
tinge of added color, the slight pressure of the fingers
on Andrew's elbow was firm and springy as a vise of
tough, light whalebone.

"Shall we stroll in the garden a moment and let
the air freshen us?"

Andrew assented, with an effort, but a fuddled
cry of "Gentian! One moment, Gentian!" called
the Doctor away for a moment and Andrew re-
mained at the window, gazing up at the sky and try-
ing to keep a sparkling wheel from whirring about
in his head.

The moonlight was bright indeed, the moon huge
and pale, the garden crowded with silver trees and
flowers. At its foot grew a single bush of Spanish
bayonet which seemed to Andrew, as he stared, the
most beautiful thing he had ever seen, for it too was
in flower, and the single stalk of waxen petals rose
out of the green spikes of the plant like a cold plume

set upon a barbarous crest. Andrew filled his eyes
with the sight of it—it seemed to him, suddenly, as
if he had run his hand into the very soil of this new
country and touched its heart. Not even the orange-
groves could so explain the nature of the land, for
they were fruitful and, after a fashion, tamed, but
this bush of thorns gave nothing to man but a single
bloom of moonlight, serene, careless and wholly
pure. More northern latitudes could not suffer such
a creation—only in the hot night of the south could
the ivory frond arise from among edged blades to
challenge a tropic star.

As Andrew considered this, he felt just on the edge
of some great discovery—some immense understand-
ing—some gift of tongues—but Dr. Gentian's hand
was lightly imperious on his arm again, and he was
being led outside to have his eyes dazzled by the
moon. The half-made discovery slipped away—the
gift of tongues was forgotten. There remained only
a leaden body and a flight of stairs unnaturally steep
and limitless, up which he was being assisted to lie
down at last in a bed that whirled into spinning
darkness.

5.

Three days later the events of that evening were
forgotten phantasmagoria, and only the shape of the
Spanish bayonet stood out distinct and fruitful in

Andrew's memory. To have been drunk in good company was nothing to be ashamed of—but the long next day in the saddle had been torment, in spite of all Dr. Gentian's solicitude—and the following one had found Andrew sober enough, but stiff and sore. The third day, however, almost made him regret that they would reach the end of their journey at evening. The air had been flawless since dawn, his first saddle-weariness had abated a little, and he had begun to notice the details of the land.

All morning they had ridden through low barrens, smelling of pine-needles—then the road had turned to swampier country, where red cane fringed the edge of the spongy bay-galls and a thrown stone went in with a sucking sound. Over languid creeks bridged with cedar-planking the road took its way— past swamps where mosquitoes buzzed and alligators slept and rotting ancient trees were hung with Spanish moss like witches' hair—then wound up into the woods again.

They had passed a woodrat's disorderly house of sticks and seen the rat run chattering up a tree with a young rat hanging to its tail. They had slept in the green russell chamber of a manor-house whose furnishings would not have shamed the Patroon and whose master entertained them with music upon the German flute; they had plucked dwarf wild-oranges from stunted, untended trees and ridden, at evening, up a grassy avenue heavy with the sweetness of

magnolia-bloom; and once Andrew had seen a cinna-
mon-colored Indian stare at them for a moment out
of the tangled underbrush with eyes black as ob-
sidian beads, to vanish among the leaves as noise-
lessly as a puff of dandelion seed. Now the shadows
were long with late afternoon, the road skirted the
river, and New Sparta was near.

"There," said Dr. Gentian as they came to a fork
in the road.

Andrew followed the line of his hand and made
out a clot of white among distant trees. "The upper
road is ours, Mr. Beard—the lower goes down to the
colony itself. You shall see it soon enough. For
the present," he smiled, "I imagine you have ridden
hard enough these last days to postpone the pleasure.
The best lands are farther down the river—that is
why you see no signs of our industry here."

"I thought you lived in the colony itself, sir,"
said Andrew, making conversation.

"Not precisely," Dr. Gentian was very amiable,
"My own house is over a mile from the wharves—
you see, indigo needs space and we have more than
a thousand souls in the settlement itself—there were
more at first but one always loses a number when
men are transplanted to a new climate—"

He chatted on, describing his newly-finished
sugar-mill and the system of irrigation he had re-
cently completed. Andrew fell more and more
under the spell of that easy, Cæsarean voice. Be-

side this man, with his tales of strange travel in the Indies and the Greek Islands, with his casual chat of the great ones of London and Paris, even Alexander Beard began to seem a little provincial. Now he quoted a passage from the Georgics to illustrate a point in husbandry, and turned from that to a discussion as to whether Dr. Goldsmith's "She Stoops to Conquer," witty though it was, might fitly be compared to the best of the comedies of Plautus. Andrew felt his own mammoth ignorance descend upon him like a heavy velvet pall and thought humbly that Lucius should have come in his place. He resolved to write to Lucius for the best edition of Plautus procurable at Garret Noel's bookshop before the week was out.

He was so engaged in trying to listen intelligently that he did not notice how the road stole away from the river again; and the goal of their three days' ride was almost upon him before he realized it. The great, white coquina house stood on a slight rise of ground, its stables and outbuildings massed behind it. There were lights in its windows, for twilight had fallen, and as the tired horses pricked their ears and whinnied at the thought of oats, servants came running out with lanterns and hubbub. Andrew knew suddenly that he was very tired and struggled from his saddle at last with the stiff awkwardness of a marionette. He was glad to throw the horse's

reins to a grinning little boy, but too weary to pay
much attention to the bustle about him.

"My dear," said Dr. Gentian and kissed a tall
woman with a proud nose and a secret mouth deli-
cately upon the cheek. "This is our young friend
from New York, Mr. Beard, my dear," and Andrew
made his manners dutifully to a worn comely hand
and words of greeting that had a foreign slur in
them. Then there was another hand, warm and
pleasant to touch, and he was being introduced to a
yellow-haired girl with eyes grey and changing as
winter cloud—"My daughter—Miss Sparta Gen-
tian." But she was not at all like his image of
Nausicáa and Andrew felt vaguely disappointed.
Then he only knew that he was hobbling up the steps
of the porch in a disgracefully ungenteel manner, but
he could not help it for each of his boots was made of
solid stone.

Strength and curiosity returned to him with food
and wine, and at last, seated alone with Dr. Gen-
tian while the Madeira passed between them the
way of the sun, he began to appraise the circum-
stances of his new environment.

"You will find we live in simple rusticity, Mr.
Beard," Dr. Gentian had said—but if these were
Florida notions of simple rusticity! It was true that
the servants were not in livery and that the dress of
the Gentian ladies was not quite in the latest mode,
but otherwise, from the old silver plate on the side-

board to the new forte-piano with Lord Kelly's Over-
tures upon it in the drawing-room, Andrew might
have thought himself enjoying the famous hospi-
tality of a Phlipse or a William Walton the elder.
That was certainly a fruit-piece by Vandermoulen
on the wall, and the Indian chintz hangings of his
own bedroom could not have been bettered at the
fashionable upholsterer, Joseph Cox's.

His eye was caught by the flash of a green stone
on Dr. Gentian's finger. There was cold, precious
light in the stone like the light at the bottom of the
eyes of a great cat.

"A quaint setting," said his host, politely, "I had
it when I served in India. The Begum happened
to think me a practitioner in the black arts." He
rose, "Shall we join the ladies?"

In the flowered drawing-room, the tall woman
with the proud nose and the secret mouth was em-
broidering upon catgut-gauze with a needle tiny as
a fairy's spear and the grey-eyed girl who was not
like Nausicáa was seated at the forte-piano, playing.
She broke off as they came in.

"I beg you will not cease your playing, Miss
Gentian," said Andrew, awkwardly, "I am devoted
to the forte-piano," he added, feeling the words were
foolish as soon as they were out of his mouth.

"Then I shan't dare continue," said the girl care-
lessly. "My strumming must sound like a rigadoon

on a milkpan to the ears of such a connoisseur—from New York—"

"Miss Gentian—I implore you," said Andrew, embarrassed.

"Oh, if you'll promise me no criticism, I'll play, sir—or sing perhaps—'tis too hot for playing alone —the piano sounds like a locust in August—heat— heat—heat—" she drummed it out on the keys, impatiently, "But sing, sing, what shall I sing? Shall it be Charley over the Water, father, to remind you of the Forty-Five—or let me see—'Bobby Shaftoe,' for Mr. Beard—'Bobby Shaftoe's come from sea— Silver buckles on his—shoon—" she hummed with gipsy impertinence and Andrew winced as he saw her eyes fixed mockingly on his shoe-buckles— "Come, fine ladies and gentlemen—what d'ye lack— lack—"

"Sing 'Beauty Retire,' daughter," said her father quietly. His eyes were intent upon hers and it seemed to Andrew as if he were witnessing some obscure and inaudible struggle of wills between them— a struggle watched by the tall woman in the chair with great weariness of mind.

"That old thing? Oh, very well—I'm a dutiful daughter. You'll pardon our rusticity Mr. Beard— we have none of your New York novelties here in songs or ladies—" She struck a chord on the forte-piano as if she hated it, and began to sing.

"Beauty retire—retire—" she sang,

"Retire—retire, thou dost my pity move
Believe my pity and then trust my love—"

Her voice was extraordinarily pure and moving.
Andrew, listening, thought of skeins of rock-crystal,
flecked through and through with tiny flakes of the
softest gold—of a golden box where a crystal bird
beat and beat its wings in trammelled, scornful de-
light. Her face had turned grave as she sang, and a
little drowsy, as if some excess of vitality came to
her through the act of singing and suffused the veins
of her heart with a sleepy power. She was like a
child now, Andrew thought—a beautiful, daunting
child—

The song ceased, and Andrew, back in his chair
again, stammered some sort of compliment. But
she would not sing again. Instead she professed an
interest in paduasoys and cordova-water and the
genuineness of the reported mode in sage-green
cloaks trimmed with ermine. Andrew, trying vainly
to remember the cut of the sleeves on the last fashion
doll from London, made but heavy weather of it.
But he did not mind, for the girl seemed to have
forgotten her obvious first intention of being rude to
him, and he was able to watch the play of her smooth
hands as she talked. Her foreign strain came out in
that, he thought—no New York girl of his acquain-
tance would have gestured with such fluid deftness.
He saw her hands for a moment as separate and

living creatures, molding Tanagra clay to the shape of a precious urn.

Then at last Dr. Gentian was offering him a candlestick and he was bidding them all good night. He happened to say good night to the daughter last of all and the warm touch of her hand went with him all the way up the stairs, as if he had dipped his fingers in quicksilver for an instant and seen them come out silvered. Dr. Gentian accompanied him to his door.

"Good night, Mr. Beard. You will find the mosquito-net at the foot of your bed a necessity. We are not so much troubled with them here as down at the colony—but they have a particular passion for strangers."

"Many thanks for the warning, sir," Andrew smiled. "Good night."

The smiling little Cæsar in black broadcloth passed down the long corridor with a wavering flame in his hand and disappeared. Andrew turned toward his own door, yawning. A spot of hot wax fell on the back of his hand—he swore and dropped his candle, which fuffed and went out. He groped blindly for it in the sudden pitch a moment and then stood up. Another will-o'-the-wisp of light trembled far down the corridor, and came nearer. He waited —perhaps the Doctor had noted his misadventure and was coming back with a new candle for him.

The will-o'-the-wisp grew and became a candle

held in the hands of a girl. For a moment he
thought, with a beat in his heart, that it might be
Sparta Gentian, but it was not. This girl seemed
about Miss Gentian's age and height but the faint,
deceptive flame she carried illuminated dark brows
and darker eyes, a skin tinctured with the sun, a
mouth ripened by it. Seen thus, in a weak halo of
light which defined no more than head and shoulders
and hands, the features were startling like those of
some worn young Madonna of olivewood in the
stone niche of a Spanish church, and Andrew excused
himself easily enough for watching from his dark
doorway.

No, she was not beautiful as Sparta Gentian was,
in the way of a golden rose, but she had her quali-
ties. The face was at once more reticent and more
untamed—the manner had an odd dignity as of one
who lives in oppression but is not afraid. He
thought of the Spanish bayonet, in flower in Judge
Willo's garden, under the swimming moon. Then
he realized with a little shock, as the girl drew
nearer, that from her dress she must be a servant in
the house, and stepped forward abruptly to borrow
light from her taper.

"Can you—" he began, but got no further, for the
girl saw him suddenly, cried out, and dropped her
candle, which went out instantly, leaving the corri-
dor a pit of black velvet. He heard footsteps run-
ning away from him and called again, but there was

no reply. He stayed futilely in the corridor for some time, cursing himself for forgetting that any serving-wench might well be frightened at a strange voice speaking suddenly out of gloom, and waiting for sounds that would tell him his idiocy had aroused the house. But the running footsteps ceased after a brief moment as if they had plunged into quicksand, and were followed by no sound at all. At first he was more than glad of this—then the continued quiet began to finger at his spine.

The girl had made noise enough to wake any ordinary set of sleepers, yet no one seemed to have stirred. And why had she cried out just once, when he first spoke to her and not again—a frightened maid in most houses would have screamed her throat dry. He stood uneasily in his doorway till doing so began to seem ridiculous, of a sudden feeling insecure and a stranger in a soft and hostile night. Then he went into his room and shut his door very carefully as if to shut out entirely the deeper darkness in the corridor. But he had an uncanny feeling that it seeped in after him, and would have given a gold Johannes to be able to find his tinder-box. Presently, though, his eyes became more accustomed to the gloom. He thought of the clear stream of Sparta Gentian's voice as it flowed over golden sand in "Beauty Retire" and hummed to himself as he undressed in the dark.

6.

The morning was so bright and calm, that he could afford to laugh at his fears of the night. He found one of the light striped-cotton suits that Mr. Windlestraw at the Sign of the Needle and Shears had assured him were all the fashion in the Southern Colonies and put it on. From his window he could see Dr. Gentian walking about his garden. The merry-mouthed Doctor seemed all content this morning, he was whistling a tune as he walked and now and then paused to smell at a flower or chirrup to a bird. He wore a broad leaf-hat and a flowered dressing-gown and looked more comfortably like the planter of Andrew's imagination. When Andrew bade him good morning, he found him observing a hedged-in patch of cactus on which tiny, red and brown insects crawled like baby ladybugs.

"Observe an industry that shames lazy fellows like you and myself, Mr. Beard," he called gayly as Andrew came up to him, "Those are cochineal insects—they have but two ends in life—to eat and make dye for our garments. I am experimenting with them now—perhaps next year we can produce the dye in quantities worth your London merchants' notice. Strange, is it not, that a little bug should carry royal colors in its belly?"

He delicately shook a few of the insects in his cupped palm and extended it for Andrew's inspection. They ran about it like tiny drops of blood, in an intent, blind busyness. Andrew looked at them with interest, feeling it strange that they did not stain the Doctor's white hand. The man was certainly a compound of the most diverse interests. Now one of the insects fell from the enclosing hand. The Doctor set his foot on it, idly. Andrew shivered.

"After breakfast you shall make the grand tour of our settlement," promised the Doctor, replacing the other insects on their fleshy green feeding-place with exquisite care.

Two things stuck in Andrew's mind particularly from that first confused trip of inspection—the babbling sound of water in the network of irrigation-canals that made New Sparta like a tropical Venice of palmetto and coquina—and the stink of the rotting indigo in the great vats in the fields where it was steeped and beaten and settled. He had never encountered such an overpowering and all-pervasive stench or such clouds of flies. "You may understand now, why my own house is built some distance from the fields," said the Doctor, offering Andrew the gilt pomander he carried in his hand, and Andrew, putting it gratefully to his nose, understood indeed.

"I don't see how your men endure it," he confessed.

"Oh—they grow accustomed," said the Doctor, carelessly. He addressed a question in lilting Italian to a bronzed statue whose naked neck crawled with

flies. The statue grinned nervously with white
teeth and replied.

"He says it stinks no worse than a Minorcan,"
translated the Doctor, smiling, "You would think
that when men came to a new country they might
give up the narrower prejudices of race—but not so.
My Italians hate my Minorcans and my Greeks hate
them both. There is always bad blood between one
or the other. Of course they intermarry, too, but
that only makes things worse."

He spoke casually, as of a herd of serviceable but
unruly animals, and Andrew sympathized with him.
The headship of a mixed colony such as this, must
be a constant balancing upon thorns, though the
Doctor did not seem bowed down. He walked
among his men with the easy grace of a beast-tamer,
and yet, Andrew noticed, with the same alert and
penetrating eye.

"But which are the Minorcans?" said Andrew,
vaguely looking for some odd, distinctive type of
body or skull, as they passed along.

The Doctor smiled. "There is one," he said,
pointing. "That fellow testing the vat. I forget
his name."

Andrew looked. Four men with their trousers
rolled above their knees and their legs stained with
dye-water were churning the liquor in the beating-
vat with a lever that had two bottomless square
buckets at either end; and a younger man, at the

side, was stooping over occasionally to dip out some of the liquor in a wooden cup and test it. Andrew caught his breath as he looked at this man; he thought he had never seen so fine a human creature. The fellow was of the middle height and seemed of Andrew's years—but so perfectly and aptly proportioned was he that Andrew felt himself clumsy and rudely-fashioned in comparison. The sun, which had fairly blackened the skins of many of the colonists, had only browned him to the deep tawniness of fine Spanish leather, his face wore the aloof dignity of a sombre prince, and every movement of his body was as deft as a gymnast's. Andrew could have visualized him far more easily dispensing justice from a stone chair of state or riding a horse to war clad in antique armor, than stirring indigo-muck. He said something of the sort.

"A good man, though sullen like most of them," Dr. Gentian agreed. "All the Mahonese are a fine-looking lot. Meaninglessly fine. The Greeks are much sharper. But that fellow knows his business. Few of them can judge a test rightly—and judgment's the secret of indigo-culture—for if the beating and churning there is stopped too soon some of the dye-matter stays in solution and if beat too long it begins to dissolve again. Either way you get bad indigo. This is the second cutting now—we hope for five cuttings this season if all goes well. The profit will mean we can finish our fort and add to the sugar-works. The fort will lie over there—it commands the wharves and the storehouses—"

Andrew looked across fields checkered with irrigation and beheld vast raw foundations of coquina.

"I should not have thought you needed so large a defensive work in a peaceable colony," he said, somewhat astonished. He had already noted the colony's guard-house with its garrison of eight bored soldiers—but this new work would hold a company, at least, and was planned for cannon.

"We had trouble here two years ago," said Dr. Gentian briefly. "The ringleaders were hanged in St. Augustine. And then—most of the Indians are peaceable enough—but Cowkeeper, the Creek Chief, is a mischief-maker. Ah, Mr. Cave," as a heavy-set man in his thirties, with a red, sweating face and odd, crumpled-looking ears, came toward them with his broad hat in his hand.

"This is Mr. Beard, Mr. Cave—the young gentleman I was speaking of before I went to St. Augustine. Mr. Cave, our chief overseer, Mr. Beard—"

"Servant, I'm sure," grunted Mr. Cave in a piggy voice and stared at Andrew intently. His eyes were a dull, hard blue, with reddened rings about them, and Andrew felt uncomfortable under their gaze.

"Mr. Cave comes from an English family," said Dr. Gentian pleasantly. "He is my right hand."

He laid his fingers on Mr. Cave's bare forearm, as if in acknowledgment of Mr. Cave's abilities, and

Andrew saw the muscles twitch an instant under that light touch.

"Dr. Gentian's very kind," said Mr. Cave defiantly. "He knows how to treat a man, Dr. Gentian does."

"Mr. Cave flatters me sadly," said the Doctor, sniffing his pomander. "He is aware how indispensable he is to us all. You and Mr. Cave must be better acquainted, Mr. Beard. We must have Mr. Cave to supper—tonight, perhaps," he continued reflectively. "Will you sup with us tonight, Mr. Cave?"

"Thank you sir. You're very kind indeed," said Mr. Cave, again with that strange rebelliousness in his voice. Andrew thought him a queer, ungenteel sort of person and wondered at the Doctor's tolerance of his eccentricities. But doubtless he made a good chief-overseer.

"And, by the way," said Dr. Gentian, amiably, "You must be provided with a body-servant, Mr. Beard—I grieve I did not think of it before. Perhaps Mr. Cave would recommend us one. Shall it be a Greek, Mr. Cave—or an Italian—or one of your favorite Mahonese?"

"Don't ask me, sir," growled Mr. Cave with a bull-like shake of his head. "They all look alike to me—the lot of them. Not one of them's worth a sucked sugar cane, if you want my advice."

"Come, come, Mr. Cave, we must not belittle our

good colonists," said the Doctor in light reproof that made Mr. Cave's muscles twitch anew. He turned to Andrew. "What preference have you, Mr. Beard?"

"I am confident that anyone Mr. Cave recommends," said Andrew, a little puzzled. Mr. Cave gave a brief, uncivil bark of laughter. "But I did not understand—I thought they were all free colonists—I mean—I did not think they would be willing to do body-service for a—"

"Oh, we'll have no trouble with that," said Dr. Gentian, briskly. "All free colonists, of course—but lazy fellows, you know, Mr. Beard—lazy fellows like most of us—" he chirrupped in tones of mock condemnation. "Any one of them would be only too glad to get out of the fields for a while and take life easy in the cool of the big house. I admit it was not my first intention to use them for such work. I had a shipload of negroes on the way—but the ship was wrecked," he sighed, "and the sea ate up my poor blackamoors—a pity—a great pity—I've not felt justified in expending further monies on slaves since then, so we've had to scratch along as best we could. By the way," he continued airily, "I understand you had an encounter with my daughter's maid last night —she's a Mahonese."

"I beg to assure you sir—it was very clumsy of me—" said Andrew, flushing.

"Not at all," said Dr. Gentian, "Don't trouble

your mind with it further, I beg of you. The poor silly girl was frightened and took you for a ghost—they're very superstitious. I assure you she won't behave in such a foolish manner again." He tapped his pomander and looked at Andrew.

"A hot, dogged wench—that Minorca piece," said Mr. Cave with ugly abruptness, and Andrew decided then and there that he definitely disliked Mr. Cave.

His behaviour at supper that evening did not make Andrew like him any better, though it did produce a certain tinge of contemptuous pity for him. The man fumbled absurdly with his food, through the meal, in a dour silence, his reddened brow bent on his plate, in spite of all the genial Doctor's attempts to draw him out. Occasionally he would steal a queer, hostile, glance at Miss Gentian and address a few loutish words to her to be repaid with an iced gentility. Andrew could not blame Miss Gentian for her aloofness, but he felt sorry for Mr. Cave nevertheless. He himself was in fine feather and described the hanging of Lieutenant Governor Colden in effigy, during the Stamp Act riots, with the devil whispering in his ear, and the unparalleled musical clock but recently exhibited in Hull's assembly rooms, in a manner to win the concerted smiles of both the Gentian ladies.

After supper they retired to the drawing room again, and again Sparta Gentian's voice breathed gold through a crystal instrument in the strains of "Beauty Retire." The occasion was marred for Andrew only by the fact that Mr. Cave had obviously taken too much wine in the interval before joining the ladies, and now sat in a brooding, red-browed silence like a stupefied bear, with his drooping-lidded eyes stupidly intent upon Sparta Gentian's averted face. When the song was ended he got up abruptly, almost overturning his chair, and without a word went over to the open window at the other end of the room and remained standing there with his back to the company.

Andrew seemed to read a message in Dr. Gentian's face—he rose too, and went over to the window himself. He stood for a moment at Mr. Cave's side—the man was staring out into darkness and did not notice him. Then he laid his hand lightly on Mr. Cave's arm to attract his attention, as he had seen Dr. Gentian do that morning.

All Mr. Cave's stolid composure dropped from him on the instant.

"Don't touch me!" he said in a fierce whisper, shaking off Andrew's hand as if it stung him, "Don't touch me, I tell you!"

"But my dear sir—" said Andrew astounded. Then he paused, for he had seen the man's eyes, and the watery madness in them. For an instant Andrew felt on his body the impact of a blow that was not given—a blow like a hammerstroke. Then the bloody color died from Mr. Cave's eyes and his mouth ceased to quiver like an angry child's.

"I—I am very sorry, Mr. Beard," he said, recovering himself with visible effort, "The heat—and Miss Gentian's singing—I am not very well with the heat and I—I cannot endure to have a stranger touch me suddenly—don't think too hardly of me because of it, Mr. Beard—"

He was almost fawning now. Andrew did not know which aspect of the man he found more distasteful—the sudden, lunatic rage of a minute ago or this present and horrible obsequiousness.

"Pray think no more of it," said Andrew, haughtily, trying to copy Dr. Gentian's tone, "Miss Gentian is about to sing again—shall we hear her?" He led the way back into the room. But he was relieved when, after Mr. Cave had taken his bearish departure, Dr. Gentian explained the reason for his singular behaviour.

"You have my thanks for treating Mr. Cave so courteously," he said gravely, "A strange, bitter creature, Cave—but loyal and devoted, so we must put up with his strangeness." He lowered his voice, "He comes of good enough stock—but you see it's by the left hand—and that frets him, whenever he's in company."

"If he had his rights he'd be rich. Rich," said Sparta Gentian suddenly in her thrilling voice.

"You were going to play us something of Han-

del's, my dear," said her father, and the girl turned
back to the forte-piano with an impatient jerk of
her head.   Under cover of the music, Dr. Gentian
went on in snatches.

"I found him in London—what an exquisite pas-
sage, my pet—very bitter against the world.   Well,
I'd known his father. A hard man. I thought per-
haps in a country where nobody knew the story—
but I fear the wound is too old and deep.   One can-
not blame him too much.   In his place, who would
not be strange?   Ah, bravo, daughter!" and he
clapped his hands.

Surely, thought Andrew, here was a gentleman of
the most comprehensive benevolence and under-
standing, and as he looked at the beauty of Sparta
Gentian's face, a little flushed now from the exertion
of playing, he resolved that the morrow would find
him more than courteous to unlucky Mr. Cave.

7.

The morrow came—and other morrows. A month
slipped down the curve of the year without Andrew's
realizing how quickly it had vanished—the indigo
was in its third cutting—then in its fourth.   Soon
it was time for hoarfrost to whiten the doorstep of
the house on Wall Street and autumn to gild and
redden the trees on the Boston road.   Here it was

hard to believe in snow feathering from a leaden caldron of sky and the cries of skaters on the black ice of Lispenard's Pond. The news from the North was scant and disturbing, but its message, to Andrew, very tiny and far away, a troubled voice hardly heard through heavy glass, the faint disturbance of cannon and drums on a ship anchored beyond the horizon.

The tea-ships had been sent back from New York in orderly protest—ships along the Northern seaboard hoisted their colors at halfmast when the news of the closing of the port of Boston came, and in Philadelphia, the bells of the churches were muffled and tolled all day. In the city Andrew had left, the Committee of Fifty One was organized and began to quarrel internally at once. The call for the First Continental Congress went forth, and from all the colonies but Georgia the delegates began to assemble. Dust-powdered riders jogged along bad roads, north and south, to Philadelphia—John Adams and the other delegates from defiant Massachusetts were received along their way with the state and circumstance of dukes or convicted felons. The Congress sat and deliberated—adopted a declaration of rights—resolved to import no British merchandise after the first of December—ended with a stately but ineffective petition to the king. John Adams found the Philadelphia ladies charming but deplored the general extravagance of the city—the Congress dissolved, to meet again the following May, having made its gesture.

A cloud formed in the sky and grew—behind it a masked and indifferent figure of chaos sharpened certain lightnings and saw that his thunders were in voice. But cloud and figure were alike unperceived by the plump, stupid king who still thought of his obedient subjects of New York Colony, and by those subjects who still stood ready to drink his health in broken glass on his birthday and wish him better advised. Only Chatham in the increasing weakness of his age saw a little—and a few men in America who had helped push a stone to the edge of a steep slope, perceived now where that bounding missile would strike in the valley, and caught their breath. But Andrew was not one of those few.

He was honestly concerned at the tone of his father's letters, however. At first they were stiff and a little magniloquent, now they grew hasty and brief, with odd gaps in them as if the writer were too constantly fretted in mind to drive quill along paper for long at a time. One strange, sparse missive had come from Lucius—he had left the house on Wall Street and the business of Alexander Beard and Son, and remained Andrew's affectionate brother, with no address. Andrew had written him at once, asking for the details of the estrangement, but had got no reply except a bundle of the more violent manifestoes of the Sons of Liberty, which he had read with a queer detachment. Lucius' name dropped abruptly out of his father's letters and was not alluded to again, while every letter was full of eager, almost querulous queries as to the details of plantation-management. Andrew pictured his father as a man at sword's-points with an invisible enemy, forced back and back into a shadow. He took his courage in both hands and wrote him formally for permission to come home—sons did that, then. But the letter he got in answer was even briefer and stranger than the rest, and adjured Andrew, by every tie of filial duty, to remain where he was for a time. "My dear Son—I implore you by all I hold most holy to remain yet a while in the Floridas—I have reasons for this request you know not of, my Dear Son—and if you would be the Staff of my Age, I conjure you to obey me in this—. Your mother is not Well and I am everywhere beset by difficulty—"

So it ran, in part, and Andrew, perplexed and sorry, could not but obey. Besides, there were other reasons for his staying. He had fallen deeply in love with Sparta Gentian and as deeply in hate with the uncouth Mr. Cave.

The first complete passion of the heart may be written in water for its permanency, but it leaves a cicatrice few care to have the wind blow on, even when iron has grown over the scar. Andrew had known women before, or their flesh, as a part of his coming of age—a circumstance of as definite, physical importance as the acquisition of a new watch by Green of London or the ability to curse a servant adequately. But the fashionable bawdy-house by the docks which he had visited a trifle shrinkingly in Lucius' company, with its ton of syrup-voiced female meat who rapped her trollops' knuckles with an iron key-ring to make them be civil to the young gentlemen, had as little to do with this present fever as the stiff exchange of high compliment with suitably marriageable daughters, minikin-mouthed, in green lutestring gowns. This was burning and ague at once, an arrow in the veins, a bitter gold in the mind.

He had realized it first some weeks ago, overseeing a gang of Greeks sickle the tall indigo with shining, leisurely strokes while the flies buzzed and the mown swathe gave out a scent of crushed herb. An incongruous moment, but most high moments are incongruous. Something had passed before his eyes like the shadow of a sea-gull in flight; then he knew; and the rest of the afternoon he had let his Greeks soldier as they would, while he stared at a visionary image through eyes that saw the field he stood in and the men who worked in that field as meaningless silhouettes cut out of colored paper.

Then he went back to the house and, after washing the smell of the fields from his body with unusual thoroughness, descended to supper and was tongue-tied and inept whenever he looked at Sparta. But gradually the first sheer bedazzlement passed, and he began to think and suffer.

He was so thoroughly acclimated to New Sparta by now that at times it seemed as if he never had led any other life. He could test the indigo in the beating vats as expertly as Dr. Gentian himself; and knew why no sun must fall upon it while it lies in the drying-shed; and the differences between the light, pure indigo called flotant or flora, the *gorge-de-pigeon* sort, and the copper-colored, heavier stuff that is used for dying woolens and the coarser fabrics. The smell of the rotting plant no longer revolted him, he had become inured to it, and if not inured, accustomed at least to the mosquitoes and flies in the fields.

He had long ago acquired his body-servant—a slim, silent, olive Minorcan lad with melancholy eyes. Also, he had begun to take a considerable interest in many of the other men and see the colony much more clearly as a whole. Some things he saw made him wince—but it was a hard-handed age, and he gradually fell into the way men have of overlooking little uncomfortable incidents that would have given him pause six months before. Whatever happened, Dr. Gentian was never to blame. The Doctor could not be everywhere, and if, occasionally he seemed to overlook occurrences that made Andrew hot behind the eyes, the abundant, evident prosper-

ity of the settlement was ample testimony for the
general wisdom and justice of his policy. Besides,
and always now, he was Sparta's father.

Mr. Cave, though, was a brute and an unpleasant
one. In regard to him, Andrew could not but feel
that Dr. Gentian carried a point of generosity too
far. The friction between himself and Mr. Cave
had begun the very morning after the scene between
them at the window. Mr. Cave was giving him his
first lesson in the ways of the plantation, and Andrew
had certainly intended all scrupulous courtesy to-
wards him. But after an hour or so of contemptu-
ous, ursine explanations on Mr. Cave's part and
eager questions on Andrew's, Mr. Cave stopped sud-
denly as they were crossing a field together.

"What did he tell you about me, last night, after
I was gone, hey?" he said hoarsely, jerking his
thumb in the general direction of the great house.

Andrew felt trapped. "I do not recall that we
discussed any one of your qualities in particular,"
he said finally. The man galled him, but he was
resolved to be civil.

"Qualities!" said Mr. Cave, scornfully. "Qual-
ities, hell. He told you I was a bastard—didn't
he now? A London lawyer's bastard without even
a decent name to his back?" His voice was vine-
gary. He looked Andrew up and down with red,
peering eyes.

"I assure you Mr. Cave," said Andrew, still grasping at civility, "that even if Dr. Gentian did happen to refer to the—the unhappy circumstances of your birth—"

"Listen to me!" said Mr. Cave with sudden violence, "You can't talk fine to me—I don't want any of your stinking New York sop! I'm a bastard, all right—I knew he'd tell you—well, if I am—" he beat his fist in his palm, "I don't want any damn cocked-hat pity from you or him neither—savvy? I take care of myself—savvy? I could stake the two of you out in the sun to dry there for boucan —savvy? All right—now you go and snigger about me with him over your wine as much as you damn well want to!"

The hoarse, brief explosion of his rage left Andrew stunned for an instant. He felt as if he had stretched out his hand in the dark and put it upon a toad.

"Oh—go to the devil!" he said, rather impotently, and started to walk away in a fog of anger. But already the man's fit had passed and he was running after him with apologies.

"Mr. Beard! Mr. Beard! I didn't mean anything, sir—I swear I didn't! I get a fit like that every now and then—Dr. Gentian knows it—he never pays any attention to it. You aren't going to tell him, Mr. Beard? You aren't going to—"

The tawdry tears were actually running down his cheeks. It took some time for Andrew, loathing them both, to quiet him with promises and assurances. Then the man relapsed into his usual heavy sullenness and the tour of instruction proceeded. But even the crowded months since then had not been able to obliterate the shoddy scene from Andrew's memory.

Then there was the time, a month or so later, when Mr. Cave had been about to take the whip to the Minorcan. The Minorcan was the fine-looking fellow whom Andrew had noticed on his first day at New Sparta, and Andrew had stopped the projected whipping in short order, for he was used to his work by then, and conscious of Dr. Gentian's favor. But again, he would not easily forget the Minorcan's clenched face as Mr. Cave had whistled the rawhide lash in his hands in preparation to strike, nor Mr. Cave's dull fury when Andrew had intervened.

That matter had gone up to Dr. Gentian and Mr. Cave had been cautioned, though, as Dr. Gentian explained, there were times when the whip—"A new colony must live its first decade under what, to all purposes, is martial law, Mr. Beard, if it is to survive. Take away the punitive power—even the power of life and death—from its governors and —well, you've heard of the first days at Jamestown—"

Andrew agreed. Dr. Gentian, as usual, had

reason and experience on his side. But he thought Mr. Cave should be discharged and said so.

"Some time, perhaps—if I could find him another post," mused Dr. Gentian, gravely. "But just now—well—we are short of men, Mr. Beard, and after all, if I did discharge him, where would the wretched fellow go? I could not turn him out naked to pig it with the Indians."

Andrew saw the justice of that, and the air cleared again. At least, he thought, the incident had been of some value, for it won him the friendship of the Minorcan concerned and he began to be popular among the palmetto-huts.

The Minorcan's name was Sebastian Zafortezas, and Andrew discovered, with that curious pleasure the mind takes in tiny coincidences, that they had been born in the same year. He began to visit Sebastian's hut, now and then—it was on the edge of the Minorcan quarter and cleaner and better kept than those of his Greek neighbors. As the acquaintanceship grew, Sebastian began to teach him Mahonese Spanish—hesitatingly at first, for he had only a little English to begin on. But soon they were really able to talk to each other—and Andrew began to learn about the deserted hut near the Altar of the Gentiles and the long sick voyage from Port Mahon.

Gradually, Andrew slipped into the way of frequenting Sebastian's hut as often as circumstance

allowed. Conversation with Dr. Gentian was always
instructive—but he found that at times he missed
the fellowship of men near his own age more than
he had thought—and Mr. Cave was the only other
possibility. Colonial and Mahonese exchanged
knives and minor confidences and began to feel
secure in each other's company. Andrew discovered
that Sebastian was passionately fond of tobacco and
repaid his language lessons with pipefuls of rank
Virginia, while the two chatted and the blue smoke
wavered in the evening air, and the Barbary ape
that Sebastian was so proud of bringing alive from
Minorca chattered to itself in a corner. Andrew
thought a dozen times of transferring Sebastian
from the fields to the coquina house, as his body
servant, but something held him back—he suspected
his friend of a pride of race as great as any
De Lancey's and feared to wound him.

They were seated so, one afternoon in early March
when work was over, smoking in comparative
silence, for both were tired. Andrew was thinking
that it was nearly a year since he had sailed from
New York, that he had had no news from home for
almost two months now, and that the little hollow at
the base of Sparta Gentian's throat was the most
lovely of all created things.

He had long ago confided his passion to Sebastian
and had received a grave, laconic sympathy in re-
turn. Sometimes he wondered at himself for re-

vealing the most hidden trouble of his heart so easily to a foreign laborer—but that ghost of snobbery was quickly laid. His friend understood him, that was enough. But he wondered sometimes, if he understood his friend.

The other had told him many things—he could see the barren island of ringdoves and eagles rise before him out of the sea, in Sebastian's words, like a city long-drowned—he could hear the soft slur of the dancers' feet in the rocky streets of Mahon —but the secret springs of Sebastian's mind remained unrevealed. Occasionally, in a chance word or a casual idiom, he could catch a glimpse of some alien, resolved purpose, hidden under the surface of Sebastian's talk like the gleam of a fish, seen far down, in very deep water, but that was all. Still, Andrew decided, he did not like Sebastian any the less for it. He shook out the dottel from his pipe, stretched his arms, and spoke.

"She is beautiful as a golden rose," he said in Spanish. "Beautiful. Is she not beautiful, my friend?"

Sebastian nodded gravely. "All women are beautiful, but only one to a lover," he said, reflectively, "It is well, so. When do you speak to her father, amigo?"

"Soon," said Andrew, "As soon as I have any notion there is hope for me in her mind."

"You must serenade her more often," said Sebastian smiling.

"No." Andrew smiled, too. "I have told you we have not the custom of the serenade."

"That is bad," said Sebastian seriously. "Guitar-music comes like a child to a woman's heart—it can enter where a man must stay out in the darkness. I would get you a guitar, my friend, if you had need of it. Tonight is a night for love and the guitar."

"That is true," said Andrew, nodding, "But you, Sebastian—how do you know? Have you never been in love?"

Sebastian regarded the bowl of his pipe.

"Yes. I have been in love," he said.

"But I've never seen you with a girl."

"No," said Sebastian. "You have never seen me with a girl." His face was masked.

"And yet—what happened, Sebastian?—Are you still, perhaps—"

"It is possible," said Sebastian, smiling. "Let us talk no more of it, my friend. Let us talk of your love instead—and wish you good fortune."

Andrew felt rebuffed, but he respected the other's reticence. Besides, it was so very much more interesting to pour his own doubts and fears in Sebastian's sympathetic ear.

"Perhaps, I will find my rose tonight," he said, tossing a pebble idly in his hand, "Perhaps."

"May you wear it many years," said Sebastian with courteous dignity.

"Dr. Gentian sets out for St. Augustine soon," went on Andrew, thinking aloud. "He will be gone some time. If I do not speak before then—"

"Ah," said Sebastian and muttered something to himself in Spanish.

"*Que?*" said Andrew, eagerly. He had not caught the words.

"I said nothing," said Sebastian, holding out his hand before the door of his hut to try the direction of the wind. "The air is heavy. We will have rain before morning. Rain and thunder."

"Nonsense, Sebastian," said Andrew and laughed. "The sky's as clear as a bell and it rained only two days ago."

"Perhaps," said Sebastian, staring into a distance. His eyes were veiled. "But for all that, we will have rain soon enough, and thunder. There is thunder in the air, my friend—thunder coming up from the sea."

PART TWO: *The Dazzling Net*

PART TWO:

The Dazzling Net

The strangeness of his friend's last speech both-
ered Andrew a little, on his way back to the house,
but not long. The gradual veils of dusk blue,
patched with silver, that evening drew solemnly
across the sky were too calm and gentle to be flow-
ered with anything more sullen than the palest
stripes of Spring rain—a cool air blew from the
inlet like a promise given in a whisper—it was,
indeed, a night for love and the guitar. Andrew
came up the grassy avenue that led to the house
with that promise clutched tight in his hand like
a Spanish coin.

Tonight, he told himself as he had told himself
so often, he would find out the color of his fortune,
black or gold. In the interval after supper, when
the Gentian ladies had withdrawn, he would speak
to his surgeon Cæsar, and know his fate there, at
least. Admitted, the Doctor was too liberal and
modern a father to give away his daughter against
her will—etiquette was etiquette—and it must never
be said in the Floridas that a New Yorker lacked
proper punctilio. But even if the Doctor did ap-

prove—what of Sparta herself? Andrew sifted a
thousand little incidents of the past few months
between his fingers like grains of sparkling sand.
Here she had certainly smiled, yes—and there
thanked him most graciously for turning over the
leaves of her new song. But there she had been
distant as a ghost, and there again, definitely satiric.
This balanced that, and left him in troubled con-
fusion. He was so absorbed in love-stricken cal-
culations that he nearly ran into one of the servants,
on the stairs, before he realized where he was.

"Ten thousand dev—," he began, in irritation,
then, seeing it was Sparta's Minorcan maid, changed
his tune abruptly. If this girl were not divinity
itself, she was blessed at least by the service of divin-
ity, and he stared at her hungrily, as if he expected
to see a golden collar, with godhead's name upon it,
around her throat. He had noticed the wench very
little after that first awkward encounter in the cor-
ridor—she went about her duties as unobtrusively
as a spirit—but tonight she seemed to him, some-
how, a precious object, and he spoke to her on
impulse.

"Is anything wrong?" he said, for now that he
came to observe her, she seemed more sombre than
usual and her face was a trifle drawn.

"Nothing, *señor*," said the girl, quietly. "Supper
will be ready in half an hour." She stood aside for
him to pass. He lingered, feeling, in the folly of a

lover, that her presence might have some sort of augury for him, if he could only puzzle it out.

"But—there is something the matter, Caterina," he went on, with vague kindliness, "You really look very tired—and the fever-season's coming on. You should go to Dr. Gentian and have him give you a powder of cinchona."

"No, *gracias*, I am quite well, *señor*," said the girl, and sucked in her breath. A dark glow came into her eyes for a second, like the soul of a flame in an obscured mirror, and died again. For some reason, Andrew felt, momentarily, as he had that evening in the corridor when her footsteps had died away so suddenly and left him alone in the very belly of night. The sensation was so acute that he almost put out a hand to steady himself against an assault of shadows. Then he remembered.

"Of course," he said rather aimlessly, "Of course —but still, you don't look very well, Caterina,— and really, now, if you went to—"

"I am quite well," the girl repeated steadily, but he saw a sob rise in her throat. It broke now, and tore her. "But the Minorcans will never have their lands, now—the Minorcans will never have their lands!" she cried, passionately, in a deep, shaken voice, and then pushing him aside with a child's gesture of impotent pain, ran sobbing down the stairs. Andrew gazed after her helplessly, reflecting that Minorcans were very peculiar. One got just so far with them—and then one came up against a blind wall of silence or an inexplicable grief. Her words were meaningless, of course, but coming, as they did, after Sebastian's talk about the thunder, they jarred him and set the pattern of the evening awry. He went to his room with a prickle in his mind, and was not pleased, when he got there, to hear, through the open window, the mutter of other voices in irritated discussion.

He was about to go out and silence the debate—the room next his was a store-room and generally only frequented by servants—when the voices rose higher, and he caught one sentence clearly.

"You've been at that wench, again," said a dry, passionless accent which Andrew was horrified to recognize as Mrs. Gentian's. "I'll not suffer it, Hilary. I'll not suffer it any more."

A low rasping murmur replied. The other voice fell to meet it, and Andrew found himself gripping the back of a chair with a clenched hand. Mrs. Gentian was so taciturn at the best of times that he had come to think of her as a statue rather than a woman—a statue whose worn, fine hands busied themselves interminably with flowers of lace and needlework, but whose memorial mouth was as dedicated to silence as the mouth of a buried nun. Now, though, those lips had opened, and a voice, arid and clear as the rattle of dry palm-branches in the wind,

spoke out a hate so weary and long enduring that
it hurt the mind.

Andrew closed the window as quickly as he could
but he could not shut out the sour, tearless repetition
of the words, "I will not suffer it, Hilary. I will
not suffer it again," or the hard rasp of the Doctor's
voice in reply. He felt very sorry for Dr. Gentian
—Mrs. Gentian had the wreck of what must have
been a great beauty. The beauty had gone, but its
jealousy, apparently, remained—acrid as the dregs
of spoilt incense. Andrew had heard, in books, of
the lengths to which such ingrown jealousy may lead
very worthy women, and shook his head in wise
acknowledgment of the strangeness of existence. It
was worse, somehow, that Sparta's mother should
yield to such a failing. He could not restrain a
natural pity for the unhappy lady, but he felt that
in combining Sparta's mother with a jealous wife,
she had committed, at the least, a serious breach of
taste.

He was relieved to find no traces of the quarrel
lingering in the air when he came down to the
supper-table. Dr. Gentian was pleasanter than
usual, if anything, and Mrs. Gentian very composed.
He marvelled anew at the deceptiveness of all
women but Sparta—he could hardly believe that the
cool, terse accents which asked him politely for his
verdict on the salad of hearts of cabbage-palm, be-
longed to the same woman whose voice had been

so sere with an exhausted flame a little while ago.
Then he was left alone with Dr. Gentian, and it
was time for him to put his question. Only now,
when the time had come, in spite of any fortification
of wine, the question stuck in his throat.

"Shall we take our wine into my study?" said
Dr. Gentian and rose, "There is a new herbal I
should like to show you—the author has some in-
genious ideas upon the domestication of the mul-
berry-tree in these parts."

Andrew assented gratefully, grasping at the
moment's relief. Besides he took it as a good omen
that on this night of all nights, Dr. Gentian should
invite him to the seldom-visited chamber which he
had always visualized as the hidden brain of the
plantation.

He took in its details now with care, as if some
one of them might give him a clue to his future.
The fantastic yet effective diversity of its master's
character was displayed in the chamber almost to
excess. It was a long, oval, high-ceiled room, hung
in blue and gold leather—the domed ceiling was
blue, as well, and powdered with small gold stars.
There were books and chemical apparatus, a set
of chessmen whose kings rode ivory elephants, a
foreign dagger with beryls set in the blade. An
herbarium stood in a corner beside the articulated
skeleton of a child—a violin lay on a carved wooden
chest, neighbored by a case of surgical instruments,

a pair of dividers and an azimuth. Yet in spite of
this litter of incompatible objects and interests, the
room gave an impression of neatness and order as
precise as that of a captain's cabin on a shipshape
frigate. Andrew felt that Dr. Gentian could go
blindfold to any single thing in the room and put his
hand upon it—and also, that the room was, in a
measure, an extension of the soul of its master, and,
should he die, would be haunted forever by a light,
sure footstep and a tight, Roman smile. He turned
over the leaves of the herbal—the plates made a
blur of color in his eyes and Dr. Gentian was saying
something about mulberries that he should listen to,
but his mind was racked, and he could not attend.

"I intended the ceiling as a planetary map, show-
ing roughly the movements of the various heavenly
bodies and the transit of the moon," said his host,
politely, as Andrew's eyes strayed from the herbal
to the ceiling, "But the work was never completed."
He sighed. "Perhaps some day, we can manage it."

"It is a splendid chamber, sir," said Andrew,
thinking of Sparta.

"It is my retreat," Dr. Gentian confided. "You
may not have noticed—but there is deadening in the
walls, and when I am secluded here, there are orders
I shall not be disturbed. I even have my own stair-
case to the upper part of the house."

"Really?" said Andrew, marshalling the facts of

his birth and worldly circumstances in proper order to present to a father.

"Yes, indeed," said Dr. Gentian. He rose and opened a door at the side—a door flush with the wall. "Would you like to see it—the workmanship is truly ingenious."

He led the way up a short, winding stair, chatting. At a landing, he paused. "We are behind the ceiling now," he said. He slid a little panel back with an oily click. "When I planned my planetary map, I thought to place my moon here and light it with a concealed lamp—a childish fancy enough, but what's life without vagaries? Then I thought my toy might burn the roof down over my head some fine night and gave up the plan. As it is, my moon makes an excellent Judas-hole if I had need of one." He stepped aside. Andrew came forward and peered through a small round opening directly down into the room which they had just left. He muttered something about an interesting device.

"Only a toy," said Dr. Gentian, "and a costly one. I fear I am too fond of toys." He shut the panel with a smooth sound, and waved into the gloom. "The stair there leads direct to the main corridor—I find it convenient, but I will not make you climb any further beyond the moon." He chuckled and led the way down again. "I have always hankered after oddities—'tis my greatest defect. I never realize how I may fatigue others with my hobbies—as I fear I have fatigued you, this evening, Mr. Beard, by your face—"

"Not at all, sir," said Andrew, untruthfully, seated in his chair again. He cleared his throat desperately. "Dr. Gentian—" he said.

"Yes, Mr. Beard?—the bottle lies with you, I think—thank you." The little gurgle of the Doctor's wine into his glass put Andrew off unaccountably. For a moment he thoroughly wished himself heartwhole and a thousand miles away. But he set his teeth and brought up an image of Sparta to aid him.

"Dr. Gentian—" he began again, with an unfortunate sense of repetition.

"Pardon me," interrupted the smiling Doctor politely, "But your glass is already full. You may not have observed it." And Andrew discovered to his horror that he was spilling a red stream on the table from an overflowing glass.

"Sorry, I'm sure," he mumbled.

"It is nothing," the Doctor assured him. "But I chance to have a peculiar affection for certain years of Madeira. Pray continue, Mr. Beard—you will find it a trifle difficult to rest the bottle on a walnut —I mention it, merely—pray continue—"

Andrew silently placed the bottle as far from him as possible and wetted his lips.

"Dr. Gentian," he said for the third time, "I

crave—I wish—May I humbly crave, sir, your permission to—"

"You may certainly have my most willing permission to pay your addresses to my daughter, Sparta," said the Doctor, briskly snipping Andrew's disjoined stammerings in two. Then, seeing Andrew's stupefied face, he threw back his head and burst into a shout of laughter.

"Why, you silly boy," he said, laughing and wiping the tears of laughter from his eyes, "D'you suppose I haven't seen where your heart's been drifting this last half-year? But the blindest worm in the ground's a crystal-gazer to a young man in love. Here, lad—" and he gave his hand to Andrew across the table. "Shake hands and don't look so solemn. You can have her if you can win her. I can say no more than that, for I won't force her —but that I'll say with a good conscience."

"I can never thank you enough, sir," said Andrew, solemnly, shaking hands.

"Well then—don't thank me at all—that's far the best course for both of us," said the Doctor, cheerfully. "I'll say this, too—the girl has no other attachment I know of, and I'll be glad to give her to you, should she be agreeable. But a word on other matters." He grew serious now. "I am not a young man, Mr. Beard, and somewhat loath to part with my one chick for the few years left me. So I must ask you this—should you marry my daughter, sir,

would you intend to remain in the Floridas or return
to New York?"

Andrew felt himself unable to think of such petty
matters.

"I have grown much attached to the Floridas," he
said, smiling. "So much that I should not think of
quitting them, if—"

"Good," said the Doctor. "Then we're agreed.
I confess—I'd feel a wrench were it to be otherwise.
Well, sir—I think that is all I wished to say. The
settlements—of course I speak merely in the eventu-
ality, Mr. Beard—had best be discussed between
your father and myself—I might even make the
voyage North in case—though in these uneasy
times—"

"My father is much interested in the Floridas,"
Andrew blurted out. "It is even possible my father
might remove some of his interests here—" He
half-regretted the words once they were spoken, but
Dr. Gentian had behaved with such admirable
candor that it surely behooved him to do likewise.

"Indeed?" said the Doctor quietly. "That is
very interesting." He reflected. "Your father is a
wise man," he said. "No one knows what this stir
in the North may lead to—but the Floridas will
stand by the Crown. And should your father—
well, well," he broke off. "There'll be time enough
to talk of that later. At present, no doubt you're
already busy with a sonnet to my daughter's eye-

brow and aching for the sight of her. Ah, youth—
what a heat in the mind it is, and how we cool when
it's over. By the way," he went on more practically,
"as you know, I must visit St. Augustine in a month
or so, and be gone some time. If this matter we
have discussed might be settled before I leave—"

"But sir—I—I—Miss Gentian—" said Andrew,
his mind topsy-turvy.

Dr. Gentian laid a paternal hand on his shoulder.

"There, lad—I don't mean to press you—or you
her—but take my word for it, the swiftest love is
often the surest and lastingest—and your bold, rapid
lover is wedded and bedded and got his child on the
maid while Sir Timothy Shilly-Shally is still sighing
outside her door."

Andrew felt this last advice a trifle frank in tone
—but it was an unsqueamish age, and he could
hardly quibble with so amiable a prospective father-
in-law over niceties of language. He went out of
the study, with the other's hand on his shoulder and
a bronze call, like the call of a centaur's hunting-
horn, in his heart.

2.

He was alone with Sparta in the garden, and his
hour was upon him. The opportunity had come so
swiftly and easily that he felt bewildered. A word
from Dr. Gentian as to the beauty of that strange

plant, the cereus, which blooms only at night. A sigh from Sparta that the house was close and she would risk any treachery of the night air for a breath of cool from the river. She had put a light shawl about her shoulders, impatiently, at her mother's insistence. In the white shine of the stars its vivid flowers were darkened and strange, it wrapped her shoulders in a pale fleece, marked obscurely with the imprint of blossoms sprung from fields on the dark side of the moon. Andrew had never seen her more beautiful or less attainable. Her composed face seemed to have no room for thoughts of him or any other man, her eyes were lighted at an indifferent planet, her mouth was a shut flower.

They had seen the cereus and marvelled—the night-flower that blooms when heaven is dark and dies in the sun, showing only the secret hours of the risen planets the perfection of its whiteness, cool, sterile and lovely as a blossom congealed from some metal slighter than foam. They had talked of a dozen, indifferent things as they strolled about. Andrew had long ago discovered that Sparta was very curious of New York and of cities in general. Her childish years were a confused memory of long sea-voyages and strange nurses. The one glimpse of London, seen when she was eleven and her roving father had been interesting Lord Hillsborough in his projects, was hugged like the ghost of a jewel

to her breast. She remembered Vauxhall passion-
ately—and the very sprigs on the dresses of the fine
ladies in panniered silk who came there in sedan-
chairs with a train of tame wits and sniffing
lapdogs.

"Sometimes, I confess, Mr. Beard—I must have
a foolish heart—I'd rather be an orange girl in the
meanest London playhouse than an empress in these
exiled Floridas. But then I remember, when I was
a child my sole ambition was to be a midshipman
on one of His Majesty's frigates so I could carry a
dirk and kill Frenchmen—and I calm myself."

Andrew longed to tell her, that he would give her
London, a chicken-skin fan, and a lapdog with the
arrogant nose of a Chinese god—but his promise to
Dr. Gentian held him back. At least, he thought,
she should be an empress in the Floridas, if he
could make her one. He glanced up the sky—the
change Sebastian had predicted was beginning.
Clouds hurried across the stars like trotting black
sheep—a rampart of darkness built itself up steadily
in the glittering wake of the moon. He chose a par-
ticular cloud. When it blotted the moon he would
speak.

"Mr. Beard—Mr. Beard—is my company so
wearisome? You have not honored me with a word
these five minutes past." Her shoe tapped on the
path. Her face was amused. He stared at her in
silence, waiting for his omen. It came at last. The

cloud blotted the moon and darkness fell on them both.

"Miss Gentian—Sparta—" he said with a crack in his throat. Then all his elaborate prologue of speech forgotten, he put shaking hands on her shoulders and drew her to him.

"Sparta? You'll marry me?" he said, in that same, cracked, violent voice. She was very near, now. He could see her eyes in the darkness, the grey had gone out of them, they were black as opals, and in each was a tiny gleaming image of his face. She looked at him steadily, for an instant, without replying. Then, "Yes, I'll marry you," she said, the crystal bell of her voice untroubled by doubt or surprise. Then his arms went round her and she kissed him full on the mouth, and he felt his heart stop in his body for that instant of felicity as if the pointed blade of the Spanish bayonet had run him through and through with a golden thorn.

Through the further events of the evening, Andrew moved like a man in trance. There were Sparta's kisses in the garden, which were real, though incredible, and there was the formal reception of their betrothal by Dr. and Mrs. Gentian, which, while equally real no doubt, seemed in memory, vague as a painting upon a dream. He could hear the words on Sparta's lips clearly enough, "Mr. Beard has asked for me in marriage, Father, and I have accepted him, subject to your consent," but of the practical conversation which followed he had little recollection. Dr. Gentian had drunk his health and called him son—he had drunk Dr. Gentian's health—Mrs. Gentian had been terse but agreeable—he was going to marry Sparta—that remained, unbelievable though it might be, the one steadfast fact in a rocking world. He tried to recall what Mrs. Gentian had said to him—her congratulations had certainly not erred on the side of loquacity.

He was sure she had said no more than, "So you are to marry our daughter, Mr. Beard? I wish you much joy," while she looked at him curiously. But then he had taken her hand to kiss it in acknowledgement and had been surprised to find it trembling. Obviously a lady of deep, if hidden, feeling —and certainly Dr. Gentian's cheery talkativeness more than made up for any curtness of hers.

He must tell Sebastian, in the morning. He had forgotten all about Sebastian till now, he realized with a start. No—not quite forgotten. He had paused an instant as Sparta and he were about to reënter the house, and glancing about idly, had seen two indistinct shapes, a woman's and a man's, part from each other in the shadows of the outbuildings. He suspected them of being lovers, and had felt friendship for them because he was now happy in love. Now he suspected more—that one shape had been Sebastian's and the other that of Caterina,

the Minorcan maid. The thought pleased him
extraordinarily —he was in that benevolent state
when we are generous enough to wish all our friends
a bliss only slightly less than our own. He gave
Sebastian a suitable wedding, engaged him as chief-
overseer on his new plantation and stood godfather
to his first child, before he fell asleep to the rushing
of light, fierce rain on the roof above his head.

3.

About the time that Andrew and his divinity
were first observing the mystery of the cereus, the
monkey in Sebastian's hut gave over its attempts
to capture a peculiarly elusive flea and began to
consider other means of diversion. Its master
was away—fleas ceased to interest after a cer-
tain time—life in general was a sucked cocoanut
and obedience a rusty chain about the body that
kept one from all sorts of pleasantly destructive
occupations. If the chain could only be got rid of
somehow—but there the monkey had never had the
slightest success before and hoped for little now.
Still, it was worth trying, and the monkey bit at
it a couple of times for luck and then squatted
down sailorwise and tugged at it till it rattled,
delightfully.

To his surprise, it seemed to give a little—Sebastian had hammered the staple in a new place that morning without noticing the rottenness of the wood. The monkey, encouraged, tried again and again, with less result, and was about to give it up and go to sleep, when one last jerk pulled the staple loose and set him free. He bounded instantly upon Sebastian's bed and sat there chattering triumphantly. There were so many breakable objects within easy reach that he did not know quite where to begin. He started by hammering Sebastian's red clay pipe against a stone. It smashed very satisfactorily in a moment or two and he amused himself for some time by carefully distributing the bits inside Sebastian's blankets. Then that too palled and he scuttled over to the door, his chain jingling behind him. The night seemed very large and interesting. There were trees in it. He had not climbed a tree in a long time.

He remedied the lack immediately, but the tree he chose wasn't much of a tree at that—it had no fruit on it to suck and throw away, with a squash, at other men or monkeys. Still, it was good to be independent again, at last. He said so at length, to the surrounding world, and set out upon his travels.

The joys of independence lasted till the first large drops of rain began to soak into his fur. Then they grew a trifle dubious. After all, he had become used to living in a house with a roof on it, and the society of mankind, while often tedious, had its compensations. He had had an adventurous outing and smelled and bitten at all sorts of new and interesting substances. He had proven himself a monkey of ingenuity and initiative. Now, the hut on the edge of the Minorcan quarter seemed snug and warm, and the food he shared with Sebastian more filling, on the whole, than what one could forage for oneself. He would go back—but he had come a considerable distance in his careless rambling and was not quite sure of his bearings.

He looked around him—ah, there was a house with a light in the window. That meant man and warmth and shelter. A different master, perhaps —but he had been so long with Sebastian that he had quite forgotten his first unpleasant experiences with masters.

He slipped down to the ground and jangled over toward the lighted house, shivering as he ran. It was really raining now, and he hated rain like a cat.

Mr. Cave, alone in colloquy with a half-emptied bottle of spirits, heard a sudden ghostly clanking through the dripping pour of the rain, and looking up, saw the Devil in person standing in his doorway with a chain wrapped around his middle. He rubbed horrified eyes and began to pray in a whisper. Then his mind righted itself and he sank back in his chair, muttering. It was only that impudent Minorcan's

draggled pet-ape—but it had given him a start, and
he did not like being startled when he was in liquor.

The wet monkey had jumped on the table now
and sat opposite him, grinning and looking at the
bottle of spirits. He grinned back at it. It would
be funny to give the miserable little beast some
liquor and get it drunk. You could get a chicken
drunk on corn soaked in brandy but a drunken
monkey would be even more amusing.

"Here," he said, splashed some liquor into a glass
and held it out to the monkey. If the monkey be-
haved itself and proved entertaining when intoxi-
cated, he might even keep it. The Minorcan fellow
set a good deal of store by it and laborers had no
business keeping pets.

The monkey took the glass trustingly—Sebas-
tian had taught it how to drink from a glass, in the
useless way men had. Now it swallowed a gulp of
what was inside the glass. The raw liquor stung
its throat—it coughed and spat in quaint loathing.
Mr. Cave roared—this was even more diverting than
he had expected. Then he felt the monkey's sharp
teeth almost meet in his thumb, gave a squeal of
pain, and struck at it blindly with the bottle.

Even so, the monkey might have escaped, if it
had not been for its chain. But the chain tangled
its feet as it dodged away—and Mr. Cave's second
blow was better aimed than his first.

He stood looking at the dead animal, stupidly.

It bled like a man. He hadn't really meant to kill it. But he had—and that Minorcan who owned it was a sullen devil. Well, he'd just have to face it out, if the ugly little swine tried any tricks on him.

He took the limp body of the monkey gingerly by one leg and threw it out of the door. It was raining hard, now—the rain would wash some of the blood off, he thought, inanely. He shivered. Killing an animal wasn't much, but he wished its hands hadn't looked like a dead baby's when he picked it up. He shut the door carefully, bolted it, and returned to his bottle. Now and then he cast an uneasy glance at the window. If the damn little brute hadn't bitten—it should have known he had a quick temper and wouldn't stand biting— His thoughts trailed off uneasily, into a mist the color of liquor.

Sebastian got back to his hut just before the rain broke, and, finding the monkey vanished, started to search for it at once. At first he did not imagine that it could have gone very far and stood in the doorway, calling, "Amigo! Amigo!" in a crooning voice, for some time. But when no chattering answered from the darkness, he became disturbed and started out to visit the huts nearest him. Even the Greeks answered pleasantly enough—the monkey was quite a favorite in the colony—but none had any news. A Minorcan woman said that she had been awakened by the rattling of a chain outside her window, but that was all.

The rain soaked Sebastian to the skin, as he proceeded on his quest, but he did not notice it. He grew increasingly distraught and cursed himself for not having seen that the monkey was securely chained, before he left the hut. "Amigo! Amigo!" he called again and again, with a dry throat, and promised his name-saint a candle for every arrow that had stuck in his flesh. But there was no answer from either saint or monkey.

He did not know what impulse drove him at last to Mr. Cave's cottage, save that he hated the man and knew the man hated him. It was there, however, in the dripping weeds near the house of his enemy, that he stumbled at last upon the body of his friend. He took it up silently, the head was still bloody in spite of the rain, and the wrinkled face stiff and sad. Then, still in silence, with the dead animal in his arms, he made the complete circuit of the cottage, trying every door and window, noiselessly. But the doors and windows were fastened and the house was dark.

He sat down upon the ground then, still holding the monkey, and burst into a fit of dry sobbing, while the rain beat on him. Then he returned to his hut.

When he got back, he lit two scraps of candle and placed the monkey's body between them. Then he stripped himself to the waist, and, going to the wooden chest that held his few possessions, took out of it a small brass medal, tarnished green by the damp. On it was the image of the Mother of God. Her face was quiet—she had seven swords in her heart. This, together with the knife that Andrew had given him, he also put on the table between the candles. He then knelt and began to pray in Mahonese. The form of prayer was one peculiar to the men of the islands and unacknowledged by Rome. Andrew would have thought him even too alien, if he had seen him then—the muscles of his stripped body trembled with the vehemence of his supplication—he was dedicating Andrew's knife to Our Lady of Vengeance. After a time had passed, he rose again, put on his soaked shirt, and went stiffly out to dig the childish grave.

4.

Next morning, in spite of Andrew's resolve, the two friends did not meet. Instead, Sparta had a wish to go riding through the new-washed and freshly-scented countryside, and when they returned, Dr. Gentian, a cloud on his brow, was dismissing a deputation of the elder Minorcans from his study. He turned to Andrew sharply, the moment he saw him.

"Was your ride a pleasant one, lad?" he said, abstractedly, "Come with me a moment—there is something I would have your advice on."

"Certainly, sir," said Andrew, pleased at being consulted. He turned to Sparta. "You'll excuse me, mistress?" he said lightly.

"I shall excuse you sir," said Sparta smiling, her fingers playing with the lash of her riding-whip.

Dr. Gentian shut the door of his study. "The Minorcans are making trouble," he said without preface. "I thought it best you should know."

"Making trouble?" said Andrew, jarred. He somehow felt that trouble at this time was an insult to his happiness and Sparta's.

"Yes," said Dr. Gentian. He hesitated. " 'Tis a long story. The gist of it's this. They say they've served their time for their lands, under our agreement. Now they want them."

Andrew's mind reverted to his encounter with Caterina on that yesterday that seemed so distant. "The Minorcans will never have their lands now," she had said.

"Well, sir—" he began judicially.

Dr. Gentian cut him off. "Yes—that was the agreement," he admitted. "Three years. But there's the religious difficulty. They're Catholics, every man jack of them—Roman Catholics. Now listen to me," he tapped his thumb on the table. "When I first took them on my ships—would they have made conditions then? No. They were starving. I took them because they were starving. I didn't think then—They let me take the Greeks because the Greek Church to our mind's a Protestant church—but if I'd proposed transporting twelve hundred Catholics to the Floridas as settlers—giving them lands—the men at Whitehall would have cracked my whole project like an egg. I had to dissemble a little—how could I refuse starving men? —I thought once they were settled here—but the present governor's my enemy, as you know—"

"Even so, sir—" said Andrew, trying to put in a word.

"See here, lad," said Dr. Gentian, very firmly and gently, "Spain's still plotting to recover the Floridas. If I yield to these men's demands and give them their lands now—the governor can make a mare's nest out of it—enough to link me up with any kind of a trumpery Spanish plot he can bogy the men in England with. Then all New Sparta falls to the ground—and who gains by it? Your friends, the Minorcans? No. I must put them off for the present—till we have a new governor—or—"

"I can see the logic in everything you say, sir," said Andrew, a trifle stubbornly, "but nevertheless—"

The green stone in Dr. Gentian's ring flashed as he stretched out his hand to Andrew.

"Have I treated you like a son, Andrew—yes or

no?" he said quite simply, and Andrew felt touched and humbled, but a little trapped as well. After all, whether or not Dr. Gentian had treated him like a son had little to do with his treatment of the Minorcans.

"You have always treated me most kindly, sir," he said, a bit grudgingly, yet hating himself for being grudging. "And yet—"

Dr. Gentian looked hurt. He dropped his hand.

"And yet you are unwilling to take my word on this—even when I assure you that one of my reasons for going to St. Augustine will be my wish to remedy the matter with the governor?"

"Of course, I must take your word, sir—if you put it like that," said Andrew, in a sudden glow of self-reproach.

"Ah," said Dr. Gentian, and laid a hand on his elbow. "Ah—that's my good lad!"

5.

Nevertheless, a tiny crack had come in the polished lacquer of his relation with Dr. Gentian. Dr. Gentian's course of action might be dictated by an expediency entirely honorable—but there must be a Minorcan side, if only a mistaken one. Andrew respected the Minorcans—they had great patience —he could not think of them as lightly aroused. He intended to find out their side—have a long talk with Sebastian—discuss things with some of the elders of the colony. Indeed, he intended much, and as people will, remained satisfied with the intent, while time drifted away, like a bough of wild peaches floating on a lazy stream.

The bright retiarius had caught and bound him in a dazzling net—now its trident poised above him and he did not fear the stroke. His servitude was too happy—why should he be free?—he ran at a golden heel.

He did not go so often to the fields, now, or to Sebastian's hut. For one thing, Dr. Gentian thought he should begin to take up the accounting and governing side of the plantation. Besides, there were expeditions for turtle, down the inlet, to be made in Sparta's company—she handled a boat like a man. There were rides through the green woods and sandy pine-barrens, and once, a dance at a neighboring plantation a day's journey away, where he saw divinity move through the stately patterns of louvre and minuet with a jealous joy. This was no New York courtship, done up in packthread stays, but something hardy and wild as a journey up the face of a crag to take the eggs from the nest of a mountain-eagle, and he rejoiced that it could be so.

Yet it seemed to him, often enough, that now, in betrothal, he was less sure of her heart than ever before. Before, she had seemed strange since she could never be his; now she was to be his indeed, but she still was strange. He could touch the hand, kiss the lips, hear the voice speak love, but in the eyes something remained aloof, a spectator who watched all that befell them both like an enchanter shut in a tower of clouded glass, without love or hate or sin, with only a dispassionate interest in the certain working of a spell. If he could once break that glass with the silver hammer of his desire— perhaps it would come with marriage and the incantation of the flesh. But the days passed, and the enchanter watched, and the glass remained unbroken.

Dr. Gentian went to St. Augustine at last. Andrew would hardly have noticed his departure, save for one thing. The Pride of the Colonies was expected with long-delayed mail from the North and might even bring an answer to the letter he had written his father about his betrothal. The letter had been written in March and it was nearly the end of May now. Then he came back to the house, one evening, after a day at the vats, as Dr. Gentian's deputy, to find his head heavy and thick, and his hands hot. He had caught a little fever, somehow, and was ill for several days.

The illness, after the first bad night had passed, gave him a chance to consider a number of things he had not thought of for some while. Sparta sent her maid to help nurse him, but did not come often herself. He was glad of that—he did not want

her to see him with cracked lips and fever in his face.
The maid was very quiet and deft—she had cool
hands, and moved without little irritating creakings
and rustlings, unlike most women.

They talked, now and then. She reminded him
of Sebastian. He had been remiss about Sebastian.
Sebastian's monkey was dead—he remembered
that, now. He had gone to Sebastian to tell him
the great news and, while Sebastian had been appre-
ciative enough, Andrew saw that he was sad. He
had asked about the monkey.

"Yes, Amigo is dead," said Sebastian, but would
say no more, though he looked at a little brass medal
that hung around his neck on a cord, and Andrew,
who was bursting with talk, had felt rebuffed. He
asked the maid about Sebastian now.

"He is well, I think," said the maid, holding a
cup to his lips. Andrew drank of the bitter infusion
within it gratefully.

"Don't you ever see him?" he said, smiling, when
the cup had been taken away.

"He asks for you often. He hopes you will be
better soon." She avoided the direct reply.

"Oh, I'll be up and around in no time," said
Andrew. "Thanks to your nursing," he added.

"I am glad if my nursing has helped you," said
the maid, rather haltingly, as if she had to hunt for
the English words. "You are a friend of the Minor-
cans—or you have been."

"Tell me," said Andrew suddenly. "What did you mean that time in the corridor when you said the Minorcans would never get their lands? Dr. Gentian is going to give them their lands as soon as the governor lets him."

"They will never have their lands," said the girl, sombrely. Her eyes fixed him. "Sometimes Dr. Gentian sits in his tall room with a gold cap on his head," she said, abruptly. "He sits there like a king—he thinks he is a king—*el rey—el rey*—" Her voice rose. "When he thinks that—men are taken into the woods to have their backs combed with steel as the coat of a horse is curried by its servant. That has not happened since you have been here, but it has happened. He had a madness in him, then—a madness that hides—the madness of a drunken king. That is why the Minorcans will never have their lands."

Andrew stared at her, wonderingly. The picture she presented was wholly fantastic, but he could not doubt the sincerity in her face.

"You're mad!" he said, finally, "Mad or—where did you ever hear such a crazy tale?"

"I should not have spoken," said the girl, relapsing into her amazing calm, "You are going to marry my mistress. I should not have spoken."

"What about Mr. Cave?" said Andrew, on impulse. "What do you Minorcans think of Mr. Cave?"

The girl shrugged her shoulders. "He is a dog," she said, quietly enough, though a bitterness colored her voice like rust. "He is mad, too—but only with the madness of a dog."

"You're not very cheerful today," said Andrew, with invalid peevishness, "And where you ever got such a farrago of nonsense—God knows I hate Cave as much as any of you can—but you make everything sound cruel."

She shrugged again. "What do you want me to say?" she said, with that even bitterness. "Life is cruel. Men that are cruel do no more than copy life."

"Don't," said Andrew, wincing, "I'm sorry you're so unhappy. You oughtn't to be so unhappy if you're Sebastian's sweetheart."

"So I am Sebastian's sweetheart?" said the girl and smiled.

"Well—aren't you?"

"Am I? I don't know. How do you know? You are a boy, sometimes—a little, little boy. You must take your medicine."

"I don't want it," complained Andrew, childishly, "You just gave it to me, anyhow."

"You must take it often." She approached him with the cup. "It takes away the fever. See, you are much cooler, this afternoon." She laid a hand on his forehead—the light touch was cool and firm as if she had brushed his brow with a ringdove's feather, fallen upon cool stones.

"There now. Go to sleep. Sleep mends the fever, too."

"Why do you say such things about Dr. Gentian?" said Andrew, impatiently, but she turned away with her finger on her lips and sat down again in her chair. He watched her through half-closed eyes, seeing again the dark Madonna in the niche of the Spanish church. A single lamp burned before it—the face was calm and secret—the face of a gypsy saint—a mystery hung above it like a dove in chains. He could feel the touch of fingers upon his brow, cool as the roots of lilies, bathed in water from the hills. He lay for a long time silent, half-drowsing, thinking of Dr. Gentian in a gold cap and a lamp before an image, and the roots of lilies steeped in a clear, cold stream.

Next morning the fever had gone; his body felt weak, but no longer possessed. He lay alone all morning feeling his strength return to him and listening with mild curiosity to the various noises of the house. The day was hot and sultry, he could feel that inside his skin, but his room was cool and he did not mind. He had a convalescent's desire for visitors and talk, but the only person he saw till noon was the body-servant who brought his breakfast, and the boy slipped away before he could question him much.

He asked for Sparta—Miss Gentian was well, but occupied, she sent her regrets at not being able to visit him till later. Then he asked for the Minorcan maid. The boy stammered and said that she was occupied too, on some work for Mrs. Gentian. He noticed that the boy seemed uneasy and as if he were listening for something in the pauses of his speech, but laid it to the heat. "Here," said Andrew, feeling generous, and getting his purse from under his pillow, tossed him one of the Spanish dollars that still passed current—the boy was a good servant and deserved an occasional coin. The boy murmured his thanks, pouched the dollar quickly, and disappeared, leaving Andrew to idleness and musing.

After a while he fell asleep and woke much refreshed. The house was very quiet and he began to consider getting up. He looked at his watch—it had stopped—but, by the light in the room, it must be mid-afternoon. A tray with food was beside him on the table—someone must have come and gone without rousing him. He was disturbed at the thought that it might have been Sparta. He called for his boy, and no one answered. Then he gave it up and set to his lunch with the first real hunger he had known in some days.

Later, he was wakened from another nap by an indefinite sound like the soft closing of the door of his room. He stared at the door—the curtains near

it still moved, but if there had been a visitor, the
visitor had departed. He could have sworn that,
in the first confused instant of waking, he had seen
a face staring in through the closing crack of the
door—a face like Sparta's, but not hers, for the eyes
in this face were hostile. A dream, probably—the
shadows had changed again and the air of the room
was charged with a heavy, groping twilight. But as
soon as he was fully awake, his decision to get up
was taken. The bed had grown wrinkled and uncom-
fortable, besides, he wanted to find out why nobody
had been near him all day.

He dressed clumsily, taking a long time. He was
not as well as he had thought, he found—the fever
had made him lax, and sweat came on his hands
when he bent to put on his shoes. However, he
managed things at last, and went over to look at
himself in the mirror. His cheeks were a little
sunken, and his hair lanker than he would have
liked, but otherwise he seemed much as usual. The
effort it was to control his body properly did not tell
in the glass. He would go downstairs now. He
would go down and surprise Sparta with the news
of his recovery.

It would be more difficult to get downstairs than
he had supposed. The main staircase looked long
and formidable—he looked at it and wondered.
Then he remembered the other, easier staircase, at
the bottom of the corridor, that led directly to Dr.

Gentian's high-ceiled study. He found it and started going down—it was dark and winding, but the steps were shorter. He went gingerly and quietly, for fear of falling. At the landing he paused, remembering, with a smile, Dr. Gentian's disquisition on the proposed planetary map for the ceiling. The panel that slid back behind the moon, must be about here—yes. His fingers found the catch. Mechanically, he slid it open and peered through the little round opening into the room below.

What he saw made his fingers shake on the latch of the panel. Sparta Gentian and Mr. Cave were seated in the study, talking. On the table between them was a pair of candles that burnt with a still flame, glasses, and a half-emptied bottle of wine.

"There's no heat in this liquor, Sparta," Cave was complaining in his grunting accents, "Why can't we have rum, you white doll?—you know well enough I'd rather have rum." His coat was pushed back, his shirt open at the throat—his whole face looked stupid and savage as the mask of a boar. Andrew saw them both very plainly, in spite of the gloom in the room. A taste like the taste of bitter aloes came into his mouth, and he felt his heart turn slowly to a dull, hard, gleaming stone.

"You can't have rum because I choose to talk to you, Charles—not watch you fall asleep with your head in your arms," Sparta's lyric voice had never been more flawed with crystal. "If the wine doesn't suit you—spill it on the floor—I'll wipe it up with my kerchief and wear it for a favor."

"By God, I believe you would," grumbled Mr. Cave, reaching out for her hand, "You're a brave wench, Sparta. Come kiss me for a brave wench."

"Not now," said Sparta steadily. "You smell too much of your wine. You've had enough kisses from me till you master the world and make me proud of you."

"You lie, you golden slut!" said Mr. Cave, and thumped his fist on the table, "I've never had enough of your kisses yet—nor likely—unless you've grown so finicky-fine this last month you'd rather have that sick cat in yellow breeches squeeze you because he sets up for a gentleman—the shopkeeping little snotty-nose! Come kiss me, I say—I want to get the taste of him out of my mind."

"You're a sweet fool, Charles," said Sparta, and went around to him. Then Andrew, glaring down at them from his spy-hole, could have groaned aloud, for he saw divinity incarnate sit down on Mr. Cave's knees like a barmaid, and Mr. Cave's red hand bend back the golden head till his mouth could settle with thirsty violence on the lips that Andrew had kissed in the anguish of a boy's first worship. The sight made him sick and faint, but he could not move away. A bleak fascination held him to the hole in back of the moon, through which he beheld, with incredulous agony, the sky of his self-made universe fall to pieces with a jangle of shattered glass and lie in broken stars in the mud at the bottom of the world.

"There," said Mr. Cave, "And there" in the pauses of his noisy embracements, "That's for every time he's paddled with your hand in the dark—and that's for every pimping New York dolly-name he's ever called you! Oh, kiss me, you jewel!" he squeaked in a sort of ecstasy, "Kiss me and tell me who you love with all your body and bones!"

"Enough, Charles, enough," said Sparta, drowsily, her voice very golden. "You know I love no man but you."

"Well, it's time and more that I heard it," said Cave, releasing her. He seemed to grow quite simple, of a sudden. His voice sank—his mouth drooped like a child's. "Where do you think I've been since you two were betrothed? In hell. In the pit of hell. They lie if they say there's no hell —I know—I've smoked in it. To see him walking with you, with his hand on your arm. You'd best be true with me now, wench." He seemed almost pleading, "You'd best be true."

"I am true, Charles."

"But you betrothed—"

She made a gesture. "Father," she said.

"I know your father," said Cave sullenly. "He's a planny man, your father. He's planned to marry you off to a fool with money ever since you were husband-high."

She laughed sharply. "My father is a lucky gentleman," she said. "He may have planned— but God sent him the perfect fool. How can anyone be so utterly a fool as my Andrew, Charles?"

"He loves you," Cave admitted grudgingly. "A man's blinded, then." He stared at his fist.

"Granted," she said, jeeringly. "But—if you think you have been in hell Charles, these last weeks —to have to take that stammering boy in my arms and give him his lollypop kisses—" Her eyes were bright with hate, "I may have to marry him yet— but if I do—"

"If you do, he'll never bed you," said Cave, in a rigid voice. "I'd have his guts on the floor first."

"No," said Sparta, with an edged and terrible smile, "He may bed me yet, Charles—perhaps—but —he shan't marry me."

"And I tell you," said Cave, starting up, with his eyes little, burning holes.

She stopped him with a gesture. "Hush, Charles," she said. "You don't understand me yet, I'd do anything for you, Charles. Sit down and give me some wine."

He obeyed, muttering. She drank the wine in a gulp and wiped her lips.

"Tell me, Charles, how soon will you be ready?"

"I have my men picked now," said Cave, in a

thick voice, "Italians mostly. They're ripe. They hate the Mahonese as the devil hates church-bells."

"And the Mahonese are ready to strike, themselves?"

"If they're not they have no bellies," said Cave, impatiently. "They've been pushed to the wall. You'd think they'd have broken before."

"Very well," said Sparta, calmly, "The Minorcans revolt. My father cannot subdue them—unless you choose. He can't get aid from the governor—the governor's against him. If you choose—"

"There's a price," said Cave, glowering. "I want you. I want the plantation. He wants his life and —I'd give him some place, I suppose. If he doesn't choose it that way—By the way—what about that lover of yours?"

"What you will," said Sparta, and smiled.

"I know what I will. But now, sweetheart, what if your father will not—"

"I would not have you too much concerned about my father," said Sparta, reflectively.

Cave stared at her. "By God, you're a cold piece," he said, huskily.

"Not to you, Charles." She rose to her full height. "I'd see you a king, Charles—not the master of one trifling plantation here."

"And who says I couldn't be a king!" said Cave, with a touch of half-drunken defiance. "Haven't bastards been kings before. What was William

Conquer but a common bastard—yet he had all England under his teeth? I'm as good a bastard as he was, any day—I can—"

"Then be a king!" she said in a voice that seemed to shake out a banner with a dragon on it above the quiet yellow spearheads of the candles. She brought her clenched hand down on the table as if she wanted to bruise its softness against something hostile and hard. "My father has money hidden somewhere—he must—you have men—strength— we could take ships—Davis did it—Teach was a fool, but Morgan did it—There are pirate kingdoms, still—I tell you this—I'll be a queen or nothing, Charles—I love you very well, but I must be a queen—I'd starve for it—I'd burn my hand in the flame for it—see—"

Her voice sank to a dry whisper, as she stretched her hand out over the nearest candle. Cave snatched it back, at once, with a terrified wordless sound. Then she was clinging to his shoulders, pleading with him, in that fierce, brittle monotone.

"A queen, Charles—they made Harry Morgan a governor—what was Spanish Pizarro but a pirate, yet he held Peru like a king—the time's not over yet—a queen, Charles—and you a king—"

But, "No, lass—no—" he was muttering unsteadily, trying to seem very bold, yet with shaken eyes, "You're trying me with talk like that—'tis impossible—I'll raise the colony on your father right

enough—I'll make you a right queen here if that's
what you want, but turn pirate against the world
and end in the hemp and the chains—"

His unsteady hand was fumbling with her hair,
trying to quiet her—she had sunk to the floor now,
and was gripping his knees, still pleading.

"Have done, girl—have done!" he said, in weak
repetition but she would not be quieted, though Mr.
Cave was now fairly sweating with discomfort and
surprise.   Further protestation was spared him for
the moment, for, on the tail of his last sentence, the
door opened slowly and admitted the tall, stately
figure of Mrs. Gentian to the curious scene.   Mr.
Cave froze at once, like a rabbit surprised by an
owl, but Sparta rose from the floor with some dig-
nity and confronted her mother.

"You fool," said the latter, slowly.   "You bawdy
little fool."

To Andrew, at his stricken post of observation,
her voice was clear and thin as the voice of a corpse
speaking from the dust, and he felt the sweat dry
on his hands as he heard it.

She turned to Mr. Cave.   "Kennel, dog!" she
said, tersely, and Mr. Cave, after one blustering,
ineffective gesture, caught a glance from Sparta,
and passed out of the room with his brow red and
his eyes bent on the floor.   Then Mrs. Gentian eyed
her daughter.

"You madam," she said, without rancor, "You

madam in gauze. What do you mean by chambering here with that lackey when the gentleman you're to marry lies sick in his bed upstairs?"

"Faith, madam," said Sparta, hardly, giving her gaze for gaze. "It must run in the blood, I think—for my father, too, has a liking for the servant's hall."

Mrs. Gentian's hand went slowly to her breast, but her face betrayed no emotion.

"You're indeed his very daughter to say that," she said, quietly, and now Sparta's eyes wavered and fell before hers. "But let it be so. I've heard you call the man you're to marry a fool."

"Do you disagree, madam?"

"Not I," said Mrs. Gentian, and laughed. "He's a puff of painted feathers—I'll buy his like for sixpence at a Punch-and-Judy. But, fool or no fool, he's rich, or his father is. Your father needs those riches—and no hot little miss like you is going to lecher him out of them. Do you understand, miss?"

"I had not thought you so greatly attached to my father," said Sparta in a stabbing voice.

"God knows I'm not," said her mother, tiredly. "But I'll not see him humbled."

"And is it your proposal, madam, that I should—"

"I propose this," said Mrs. Gentian. Her hand fell upon Sparta's shoulder and held it. "If this ninny you're to marry once knew what's passed be-

tween you and that lawyer's by-blow—he'd throw
you aside like an applecore for all his ninnyishness.
You must fasten him to you by his ninny's honor
or lose him. You'll have him in your room, miss—
as soon as he can walk—oh, I'll trust you for that
—you have ways that would blind a sailor—but
that you'll do. After that—" Her smile was an
East wind. "Let him marry you or keep you—it
matters little—we have him in a yoke."

Andrew could bear no more. He shut the panel
with fumbling fingers and somehow got up the
stairs and back to his room. When he reached there,
he found the Minorcan girl, just done with tidying
his room and about to leave. She gave a soft cry
as she saw his face.

"Oh, go away, go away!" he sobbed wildly, as he
flung himself into a chair and put his head in his
hands. "Go away and pray for me, Caterina—
I think I am the unhappiest man in the world!"

6.

Andrew lay on his bed, staring up at the ceiling
with tormented eyes. He had thought he had known
shock before, when his father's easy voice abolished
the Beards of Westmoreland with a sentence. But
that half-forgotten wound in the vanity of youth
seemed like a wound in silk to this present pain.

Again he felt the solid floor of life turn under him dizzily and alter—but this time it did not merely change, it blackened while he looked at it to the color of corrupted silver and soiled thunder walked in iron wherever he could see. The knowledge of good and evil had descended upon him at last, and he lay excruciated beneath it, like a harper crucified upon the strings of his own heart.

That his pain might well have seemed unnecessarily acute to any dispassionate observer would hardly have consoled him, had he known it. He saw the whole world now as a lie, which it was no more than it ever had been. But circumstance had mixed in him the fool and the gentleman—qualities both somewhat in disrepair nowadays—and at present, no doubt, the gentleman was somewhat sunk in the fool. The cold brain of heaven, whose thought is a falling star between illusion and illusion, might properly regard his adolescent strugglings with befitting contempt but that task of scorn may, perhaps, be left to it.

A certain, stale equanimity returned to him at last. He was still dazed and shaken but he began to think. At one moment he was quite confident that what he had seen in Dr. Gentian's study was merely a nightmare of the mind—at another that Sparta, for some inexplicable reason, had been playing a game upon the sullen Mr. Cave. But truth seeped in gradually through his defenses and at last he stood ready to accept the fact.

Seen clearly, the situation was only too plausible. He had often thought humbly enough, that it was strange that Sparta should love him, and strange that she should never have loved before. Well, she had loved before, that was all, and if she chose to garland an ass with roses, such was her prerogative. It seemed curious to Andrew that this wise and reasonable thought brought him so little relief. He began to consider just what there was to be done.

He must get away from New Sparta. But then he shuddered—he and Sparta were still betrothed, as much as they ever had been, he remembered with sudden pain. It hardly lay with decency to call her a slut to her father's face—yet what other reason could he give for so sudden a departure? Then there was Mr. Cave's mad plan of an uprising in the colony—a driving of the Minorcans to revolt. Admitted, he now owed Dr. Gentian little but the hate of a bamboozled sailor for his crimp—the Minorcans were still his friends—Sebastian—he could not go without warning them. Now indeed he felt a net on his body and struggled at the cords in futile disgust. His struggles were interrupted by a light knock at the door. He called. The door opened. Sparta was there.

"Why Andrew, dear," she said, looking at him in affectionate surprise. "I thought to find you still in bed with the fever and bring you your supper. But you are well again—and I am so glad."

Her voice was the same dropping skein of gold-and-crystal that he remembered—the same enchanter slept in her eyes.

He looked at her a long time. No, he could not talk to her now.

"My fever's gone," he said at last. "I think I'll come down to supper, if you'll call the boy to lend me his arm."

7.

He was sitting at table in Dr. Gentian's chair. The room had not changed its aspect—the fruit-piece by Vandermoulen still hung above the sideboard where silver glimmered in the candleshine. The ladies he supped with took peaches from a bowl and peeled them delicately with silver knives. There was no mark upon their white hands like the mark of a bloody paw—the wine in the decanter at his elbow seemed excellent St. Lucar,—he could savor its bouquet quite naturally. That was odd, thought Andrew dully, as he ate and drank and talked. He felt vaguely that things should have been different —more in keeping with the tiny, persistent sound that tapped like blood flowing from a wound continually inside his head. He had yet to realize that tragedy may occur in a bandbox and that horror

needs no set apparatus of skeletons to make the
bones feel cold.

It was odd too, that he should be eating and
drinking. He watched his knife cut a piece of
meat, his fork carry it to his mouth. The hand
did not falter at all, nor the throat refuse to swallow.
All his muscles obeyed him handily—it was clever
of them. He could question and reply in a normal
voice—he found himself listening with every appear-
ance of attention to a long, tedious account by Mrs.
Gentian of some customs of the Spaniards in St.
Augustine.

It appeared there was one called "Shooting the
Jews." On the Saturday morning after Good Fri-
day, when the bells rang hallelujah from the Cathe-
dral, the Spanish inhabitants would shoot at straw
dummies labelled Judas and Caiaphas, hung up at
the corners of certain streets. Really, how interest-
ing, he heard himself saying, while privately he
searched Mrs. Gentian's calm face for any signature
which might betray that she had been born in hell
and was surprised to find none there.

So the servants went and came, and plates were
laid and removed, with the passage of innumerable
minutes, till the world grew old and white and tot-
tered upon a dry branch like a dying cripple, and a
stone hardened in Andrew's breast, and three people
sat enchanted around a long table, peeling peaches

and putting the flesh of peaches in their mouths. At last it was over, and he was left with his wine.

He arranged nuts on the table, very carefully, in a cross, in a square, in the initials of his brother's name. His mind seemed to have room for nothing but the exactitude of their patterns. He could think consecutively no longer—he was tired of thinking.

A nut rolled away from under his hand, and he cursed it whiningly and replaced it in its design with nice deliberation. Presently he would go up to his room with the India chintz hangings, and, if he had his wish, would die among its printed flowers like an insect crushed between leaves of painted paper. But that would not happen—people did not die as easily as that.

Mrs. Gentian and Sparta had watched each other all through the meal like cat and cat. A detached part of his consciousness told him that now, in the lifeless voice of a boy repeating a dull lesson. And, for once, Mrs. Gentian had seemed the stronger of the two. Did that mean anything—if it did, he was too tired to think what it might mean.

Presently he was pleading fatigue to the ladies and climbing the stairs to his room. The shadows wavered in the corridor before his candle. He wished, vaguely, that he could see that Minorcan girl, now, as he had first seen her, coming toward him like the image of a barbarous saint walking the sea, the light of a single candle ghostly upon the darkness of her brows. But even if she did come, she would turn to something evil as soon as he touched her. All things turned to evil the moment they were touched. There was evil in the very particles of the air, an impalpable dust of black glass, and people took it into their lungs and turned into dolls of spoilt straw and rotten leather that fell to pieces as they moved.

Sebastian's thunder was coming. He could hear it growl in the distance like a dog on a chain. The thought of the bright blade of lightning gave him a little ease—that at least was clean, and could run sick arrogance to the heart.

He was sitting, still dressed, in a chair in his room. Time had passed, but how long a time he did not know. The candle on the table burnt unevenly, with a smoky flame. The house was quiet —the thunder nearer at hand.

He passed his hand over his forehead and tried to collect his thoughts. The heat in his brain like the throb of blood from a spent artery, had eased a little now—he was still in stupor, but the weight of it was not so extreme. He began to realize that, whatever else might have happened to him, the fever was not yet wholly gone from his body. He must sleep—after he had slept, the beat in his head might stop.

He was about to rise when his eyes were drawn to the door. It was opening—a crack—a gap—letting in soft blackness. He stared at it, without fear or surprise. It might be Death—if it were, he would not lift a hand.

A hand, a bare arm, came slowly out of the darkness. The hand held a white flower between its fingers. It was Sparta's hand.

After what seemed a long time, "Andrew," said Sparta's voice, in a low call. He shut his teeth and would not answer. There was silence, while the hand moved a little and the curtains waved in the draft. Then, "Andrew," said the voice again—the fine gold streaking the crystal with threads of radiance. Then hand and flower were slowly withdrawn and the door closed gradually, leaving Andrew staring like a blind man at where they had been.

His pistols lay on the table near him, in their case. He took one of them out and examined it slowly, with minute care. The priming needed to be changed—this damp weather ruined one's priming. But he made no move to change it. He fiddled with the trigger a moment, a childish look on his face, not thinking of anything; then he forgot why he had taken up the pistol, and stuck it in his pocket to get it out of the way. His hands relaxed—the spinning in his mind began to slacken, like a top running down.

After another while, he rose, stiffly, and smiled. The stupor had passed from him—he knew what he would do. If the world were colored like a bat he would take the color of the world. He would take the instant of brisk desire for the image seen in a cloud and know in its entirety the damnation of possession and the wittiness of the flesh. He would despoil as he had been despoiled and lose the rags of gold he had brought from fool's paradise in the quick heat of the blood as a wise man should.

A sudden glare of heat lightning showed his face to him in the mirror. It was haggard and strange, but he smiled at it and went to the door. Down the corridor, packed with bags of darkness, lay another door with a white flower before it, and he was going there to sleep with a ghost.

PART THREE: *The Pit of Oppression*

PART THREE:

The Pit of Oppression

All along the corridor, utter night lay reclined like the body of a great, black cat, asleep with its head on its heavy paws. He went softly—to his dizzy mind it seemed as if at any moment his feet might sink into dark, sleek fur and a bristling, gigantic back hump up uneasily beneath them. The corridor seemed much longer than it did in daylight —why had he blown out the candle in his room? He had come some distance and still he could see no door with a white flower before it—he must have passed it, somehow, in this place where darkness was a mask of black satin across the eyes.

He turned about, as he thought, and started to grope his way back, with his hands out before him. They touched against a wall. He grew confused and stopped, trying to fix the points of the compass in his head. He turned again, walked forward and came up against another wall—the corridor was gone—he was trapped in a narrowing box of velvet and ebony whose sides shut in around him like a closing fist. The ludicrous aspect of the situation did not strike him—he had passed beyond humor—

his mind was a sharpened point that had given itself
entirely to the pull of a dark lodestone and now
wished with all its strength to touch that lodestone
and cease. He stood perfectly still for a long
moment before the unreasonable wall that had so
suddenly risen up in front of him, angry, ridiculous,
impotent, and more than a little afraid.

Ah, he had it at last. He turned to the left and
moved forward — right — the wall was gone.
Sparta's chamber must be farther along, on the other
side of the cross-corridor—he would find it now.
A sound would have helped him greatly—but there
was no sound at all in the buried world through
which he moved but thunder rattling the iron roof
of heaven and the creeping noise of his own shoes.
No, wait a moment. There was another sound.

There was another sound, faint and distant, as
if it came through mufflings of black wool, but dis-
tinct enough when he listened for it, a sound made
by some creature in pain. He paused and listened
intently. At first he could not fix its direction. It
seemed to come at once from everywhere and from
nowhere, as if the encompassing and shadowy air of
night itself were whispering to itself in quietness a
single, monotonous word of obscure anguish. Then
at last, after much time, he traced it down. The
sound came from above, it was the voice of the
Minorcan girl, and she was calling "Water, water,

water," very slowly and weakly, as if her throat were small with pain.

He stood irresolute for a few seconds, the blood thudding in his head. Something hot and stinging began to die from his veins. "Water, water, water," said the thread of breath from above, in desolate supplication. He remembered a mole he had seen once, after dogs had worried it—it lay on its side, half-dead, and made much the same feeble, pitiful outcry, thin and incessant as the creak of a locust. He had been ready for desire and hate—for Death playing knucklebones with his joints in a corner— but for this he had not been ready. He could not go to Sparta with that haunted outcry in his ears.

He turned again, and bruised his shin against the bottom step of a stair. He knew where he was, then—he had strayed into the cross-corridor by mistake—the servants' quarters were above. "Water," said the voice, and choked. He started to climb the stair.

The thread of voice led him to a closed door. He tried it—it was locked but the key was on the outside. Then, just at the point of unlocking it, he paused. What was he doing here—he was looking for another door, a door with a flower before it. He had not come all this way with a black hand muffling his face to comfort a serving-wench in the throes of a bad dream. He started to turn back, but as he did so, "Water," said the crucified voice again, and the accents were not those of an imaginary anguish. He cursed himself for a fool, and turned the key.

At first he could see little in the room but the pale square of the window. Then, outside, a jagged thornbush of lightning flowered for an instant and vanished, and in its abrupt glare, brief as the flashing of powder, he saw the Minorcan girl standing upright against the foot of her bed. But now she seemed much taller than he had thought her. She was standing on tiptoe—why was she standing on tiptoe, and why were her arms stretched up stiffly over her head? Then she gave an inarticulate groan and he realized, with a shock, that she was bound, and suspended from the ceiling by a cord tied round her wrists so that the tips of her toes just brushed the floor.

He ran over to her and tried to lift her up in his arms. She gave a moan of relief or pain and her head drooped suddenly on his shoulder. Then he was trying to raise her with one arm and pick at the knots in the cord with his other hand. "Knife," he kept whispering to himself, inanely, "Knife. Knife. Knife. Where's knife?" It seemed hours before the knife was out of his pocket and the cord frayed apart.

He caught her in his arms. Her body was loose and heavy as the body of a rebellious child—she had fainted with exhaustion and pain. Staggeringly, he lifted her on the bed and laid her down as comfortably as he could. She stirred a little and sighed. "Agua" she said, in a whisper. He found some water in a ewer, splashed it clumsily on her face, wet her lips with it. Outside the thunder grew fainter and rain began to fall in a black, streaming torrent. He did not notice it. He knew only that he would never breathe easily again, if he did not bring back to life, if but for an instant, this slight, defiant flesh, austere now, coldly wrapped in the husk of a darker flower than Sleep's.

She came back to consciousness, grudgingly, like a child learning to walk, like a visitor long-detained by a gift of pomegranates at a stony threshold and still half-unwilling to return. At last she was strong enough to sit up and make the woman's automatic gesture at arranging her hair.

"Thank Christ," said Andrew, shakily, hardly knowing what he said, "I thought you were dead."

"I was dead," said the Minorcan girl, and smiled a little, "How did you know?"

"I heard you—in the corridor—you were crying—"

She bit her lips. "They hurt my hands," she said, looking at them. "They hurt my hands."

"Who did it?" said Andrew, voice and body cold.

"She said I was her husband's strumpet," said the Minorcan girl, her eyes very black in the darkness. "She said she'd teach me. Then she got Mr. Cave."

"I think I shall kill Mr. Cave," said Andrew. "But your—the other servants—they must have heard—Good God—the key was in the door—"

"They are Greeks," said the Minorcan girl. "Touch a Greek and you touch a rat. Besides—they are hers and Mr. Cave's."

"They are devils," said Andrew, sobbingly. "This is a house of devils—oh, a house of devils—"

"Listen," said the Minorcan girl, with that smile that set her apart from him, in a circle of antique and savage stones. "Even yet, you do not know." And, sitting on the bed, while the rain slashed at the window, and Andrew dabbed at her bloody wrists with a torn handkerchief, she began, quite quietly, her recital of five years' wrong. There was no passion in the sentences—if there had been Andrew felt he could have borne their impact more easily. There was only the calm, insistent pulse of her even voice, throbbing slowly in the darkness like the beating of the wings of a tired bird.

"So they hanged the priest in his robes, on a wooden post, and stuck a piece of bread in his mouth to mock him," her voice tolled gravely. It was the unforgiveable sin. "After that—"

"Oh, for God's sake, Caterina—for God's sake—" stammered Andrew, excruciated beyond his strength, "Can't we get away from this house—tonight—in the rain—they can't hear us in the rain—there are horses in the stable—we'll ride to St. Augustine—

tell the governor—he'll help us—my father's rich —we'll take Sebastian, too—Oh, come, Caterina, come—" He was pulling at her hands. She clenched her teeth, and he realized that he had hurt her.

"How can I ride, with my hands?" she said, helplessly.

"I'll tie you to the saddle—you can ride pillion behind Sebastian or me—you must, Caterina—you must—we can't stay here any more—" He was pleading with her now, as if for some salvation of spirit that lay hidden between her hands like a coral amulet. Her face was serene as she listened. She made a little gesture.

"Wait," she said, and rose from the bed. When she was on her feet she swayed for an instant. "Ah, Dios," she said, under her breath. Andrew offered her his shoulder, but she put him aside and walked slowly over to the other end of the room. There was a little shrine there—a cheap, plaster image of the Virgin. Her robes had been gaudily colored in staring blues and reds but they were mildewed now and the colors were faint and gentle. A tiny wick burned in a small cup of rancid oil at her feet. Caterina sank to her knees.

"*Madre de Dios*—Mary Virgin—Tower of Ivory —House of Gold—" she began, in Mahonese, in a soft, lulling voice. Andrew watched her perplexedly from the bed. The scene touched him with pity and grief, but it was something he could not understand. He would have been glad enough to kneel beside Caterina himself and pray, if he had thought it would bring her any comfort, but there was something in the absorption of her eyes, as she gazed at the tawdry little doll with a tarnished crown, that made her incomprehensible. It belonged, with the flower of the Spanish bayonet, to an earth that was not his—an earth in which he would always be a stranger. And yet, as the mutter of the prayer went on, he knew that he did not wish to be a stranger to that alien, enchanted ground.

When Caterina had finished, and crossed herself, with head bowed, she came back to him.

"Yes. I will come," she said. Their eyes met— for an instant he seemed to see behind hers, into her heart. There was a message there, clear and pure as if air had written it on a tablet of mountain-snow, but a message he could not read, for it was written in her language, and to him the characters of that language were mysterious as marks carved upon a druid stone. He stared for an instant, vainly— hoping for a Pentecost that did not descend. Then the veil fell between them again.

They crept down the stairs together, hand in hand, like children afraid of the dark. When they got to the long corridor, she turned to go down it but he held her back. "No. Not that way," he said. He felt suddenly as if he could not bear to stumble past the door with the white flower, even to get his other pistol and his father's letters. He was in a torment of impatience to leave the coquina house behind him forever. There must be arms in Dr. Gentian's study—besides, there was less chance of arousing the house if they went through there.

He smiled. The high chamber with the gold stars in its ceiling which had seen his imaginary Eden crumble to ash should be the instrument of their deliverance from this house of pain. He led the way slowly to the hidden stair.

When they had reached the panel behind the moon, an instinct of precaution made him slide it back and look. So, for the second time that day, an odd vision was vouchsafed him.

Dr. Gentian stood in front of the fireplace, warming his hands. He must have been but newly come from the road, for his muddy boots were set in a corner to dry and his riding-coat, stretched out on a chair before the fire, was streaked and spattered. He himself, however, was as neat and trim as ever. He had changed his muddied coat for a loose dressing-gown and his boots for soft Moorish slippers, worked with gold thread and turned up in stiff petals at the toes. On his head was a turban of yellow silk, such as many gentlemen who had served in the Indies affected, and he rubbed his hands over and over each other like a fly cleaning its wings, as he talked to himself in a low, quick voice and smiled at the fire.

Andrew could feel the Minorcan girl's whole body shudder against his for an instant and then grow still. "The gold cap!" she whispered in the voice of a beaten ghost, "He has on the gold cap. We shall never get free of him now."

"Nonsense," said Andrew, though he too was oddly affected by the sight of that spruce, quaint figure crowned with an inverted tulip-flower, smiling dimly and talking under its breath to a burning log. "We'll take the other stairs." He shut the panel and started to go back. But a few steps away from the upper door, he stopped and listened. There were footsteps in the corridor, a light step and a heavy one, going to and fro like the pace of sentries on guard.

"They are looking for me already," said the Minorcan girl, slowly, with a calm despair.

Andrew hesitated, feeling the lips of a velvet trap close slowly upon them both in the narrow darkness. Then he made up his mind. Better face Cæsar in his study than chance what might be in the upper corridor. His mind stuck on the thought that the house had orders not to disturb the Doctor when he wished quiet and that there was deadening in the walls of the high-ceiled chamber. His hand slid to the butt of his pistol—he had never killed a man—what was it like when you killed a man?

He saw Cæsar sprawled in front of the fire with blood on his neck—a little flame stole out shyly from a log and licked at the yellow turban. He shivered. Fool, he was wasting time. "We'll risk it," he said hoarsely, and went sneaking down the stairs again.

At their foot, he paused. The Minorcan girl was on the step behind him—he could hear the flutter of her breath. Beyond, in the study, was another sound—Dr. Gentian's voice, plainer now.

At first Andrew thought some one else must have come into the room—the Doctor's tones were the tones of a man talking intimately to a familiar friend. He put his eye to a crack in the door. He could see little, but no other form than the Doctor's crossed the range of his vision. Then he realized that though the Doctor's voice questioned and affirmed and at times even pleaded, as if the friend he addressed were a superior in rank, there was never any reply.

The voice went on and on. "I saw Baron Funck in London," it said. "He took me into a room full of silver candlesticks and swore he would show me a secret, but the only secret he showed me was a juggler's trick. Then there was Hauptzehn in Dresden—he had Lully's book but he did not have the key. The Rose-Cross is nothing—they pretend to make diamonds but they do not know the writing on the wall of the tabernacle or the tears of the

Golden King. In India I have seen the man climb the rope and the flower rise from the dust and go back again—I have seen the basket thrust through with swords—but I wish more than that. Am I not an Initiate? Have I not heard the goat cry in the dark and scattered the herb in the fire? I cannot seek elsewhere again—I have grown too old." The voice had a note of chant, now. "There is something buried at the roots of the mountains—why can I not put my hand on it? Bacon had the knowledge they say—am I so much less wise? I will not fool myself with crystals and black wafers—these things are folly, but there is something left—something beyond the speculum—behind the glass. I will give my soul for it, I tell you—I will give my soul for it." Now the tones were those of a merchant driving a canny bargain. "I can give you a thousand souls. You are foolish not to bargain with me. Come out of the fire, Baphomet—Baphomet—Baphomet—" the voice reached a shriek of supplication, "Come out of the fire, Baphomet, and buy my souls!"

Through his crack, Andrew saw the yellow turban waver and droop in fatigue like a crocus beaten by the wind. Now. He flung open the door and stepped into the room with his pistol clutched tight in sweating fingers.

The shock of his abrupt appearance, to a gentleman who so obviously expected other visitors, must have been painful in the extreme, but Dr. Gentian bore it with admirable equanimity. He put his hand to his mouth once, slowly, while his face altered. Then he came forward to Andrew, smiling, with hand outstretched, as if the pistol presented at his heart had no more importance than a sprig of rosemary.

"Ah, Andrew," he said cheerfully, "I had hardly hoped to see you before the morning. Come over by the fire, lad, and warm yourself—the house is chilly with the rain."

"Keep your distance," said Andrew hoarsely, "Keep your distance, you miracle of hell, or I'll shoot your heart out."

Dr. Gentian's hand dropped to his side. He looked puzzled and distressed.

"Why lad," he said gently, "Are you still so fevered?" He smiled sympathetically, "Or did my playacting just now fright—how much did you hear of it?" he said in a swift breath.

"Enough," said Andrew wretchedly. "Keep your distance, Dr. Gentian—I have no wish to murder you, but I leave your house tonight."

"I forbid it," said Dr. Gentian, promptly, "As your physician, if not as Sparta's father." He came a little nearer. "Let me look at your eyes, lad—yes, they're bright." He shook his head. "Far too bright—and your pulse is beating like a hammer I'll warrant, and your skin—oh, I know the signs!

It would be madness for you to ride in this rain—"
with each phrase he approached a trifle, delicately,
on slippered feet.

"Let me feel your pulse a moment, lad," he said
now, stretching out his hand again. Andrew beat it
down with a gesture.

"Stop," he said, "I know you. The lot of you.
You've plucked me like a pigeon between you—
you and your whory daughter and your wife that
hangs up servant girls by the thumbs. You tor-
turers. Come out, Caterina," he said, without turn-
ing his head.

The door in the wall opened, the Minorcan girl
stepped into the room. Dr. Gentian gazed at her
for a moment. A tiny drop of blood gathered on
one of her wrists and fell. Andrew, looking at the
Doctor, thought he seemed more like a Cæsar than
ever, with the color out of his cheeks, but this time
he knew the face. It was no Julian or Augustan
coin—it came of a later mintage—the silver was
debased—the lids of the eyes grown heavy. Calig-
ula at the Games staring down at a bloody sand,
where something moved and cried—Tiberius killing
flies like so many black slaves at the window of his
villa above the cold, star-amethyst of the sea . . .

The Minorcan girl shut the door slowly behind
her. She held out her bloody wrists. She did not
speak.

"So," said Dr. Gentian, sucking his breath in.

Then, without warning, he sprang for the side of the fireplace and pulled at the bell-cord furiously. The hammer of Andrew's pistol fell. The fire sparked in the flint but that was all. He remembered looking at the pistol, years ago, and thinking it should be reprimed.

"Oh, Christ," said Andrew, with a sob, and leaped forward, throwing the pistol aside. He heard the Minorcan girl cry out. Then a flare like the sudden flare and extinction of a puff of red fire lit the base of his brain for a moment and was succeeded by sparkling darkness.

When he roused, his head felt huge, and as if it would split apart like a cut orange at the slightest movement. He was propped in a corner with his hands bound behind his back and Mr. Cave was standing over him with a gorged, pleased look on his face.

"He has a skull," said Mr. Cave, turning away from him to the Doctor, who seemed engaged in washing his hands in a little basin, "I couldn't use my right hand, but even so—by God, all the time you were bandaging him, I thought you were wasting lint." Andrew noticed now that Mr. Cave carried his right arm in a sling. Dully, he wondered why.

"You were admirably prompt, Mr. Cave," said the Doctor, aloofly, drying his hands, "I must thank you. I confess, I have seldom known you so prompt before."

Mr. Cave's face grew sullen. "We were looking for the Minorcan piece," he said, "I thought she might have come down your stair. I heard you pull at the bell as I got to the door."

"A fortunate coincidence," said Dr. Gentian reflectively. "And yet—in future, Mr. Cave—unless by my invitation—"

"I wouldn't have used your damn staircase tonight," said Mr. Cave, flushing, "But I thought—as long as she'd broken away—"

"Quite right," purred the merry Doctor. "You are always right, Mr. Cave."

"What have you done with her?" said Andrew, thickly. His senses were returning, he felt on the point of vomiting from the warm, luke, jellyish taste of blood in his mouth.

The Doctor eyed him with his head cocked on one side, like a bird.

"Do not vex your mind unduly, Andrew," he said, "Your trollop has gone back to her room. She will doubtless undergo a little discipline in the morning, but that is all. I shall not even put her back in the fields."

"May God damn your soul in hell," said Andrew, retching, "If I could only get loose—"

"You would merely do yourself an injury," said

Dr. Gentian briskly. He turned. "You sent for the soldiers, Mr. Cave?"

"Yes, sir," Mr. Cave grinned. "They'll have work to do for once."

"Ah, yes," said the Doctor, "By the way—" He picked up an object from the table, daintily and came over to Andrew, holding it at fingers' length. "Do you recognize this, my boy?"

Andrew stared at the object. It was the knife he had given Sebastian, but now there were rusty stains along the blade.

"Yes. It's my knife," he said. He was about to add that it had not been his for three months, but did not because each word he uttered was a stab in his head.

"Thank you," said the Doctor, "That is very satisfactory. You see, Andrew, your Minorcan friend, Zafortezas, happened to stab poor Mr. Cave in the arm with that knife a few hours ago. A flesh-wound only, fortunately. Your knife. Curious. And the same evening, you, for some inexplicable reason, attempt to murder me with a pistol. It begins to look like a plot, Andrew—it begins to look like a plot"—and he shook his head sorrowfully, while his eyes danced with little points of light.

"You—" said Andrew, raging impotently.

"Yes, Andrew. A plot to take my plantation

from me.   Ah, Andrew, Andrew, I wouldn't have believed it of you," he said.

Andrew was silent, feeling unmanly tears of weak fury prick at his eyes.   Then he thought of something.

"I appeal to the governor," he said.

"Inadvisable," said Dr. Gentian.   "The governor may not be my friend—but I doubt if he would give much weight to any appeal from a Northern rebel."

"Rebel?" said Andrew, dizzily.

"Rebel.   Oh, I forgot—you have not had your mail.   Well, you may take it to jail with you, and read it there.   Yes, Andrew—the Northern Colonies are in revolt.   There's been blood spilt—" He tossed a packet of letters into Andrew's lap.   "Most interesting—especially the one from your brother. He seems to be deeply involved in the rebellion. Your father is greatly concerned."

Andrew was struck dumb.   So it had come at last. He saw his brother Lucius firing at a man in a red coat—his father sitting at his desk in the home on Wall Street with a newspaper crumpled before him and his eyes looking into a darkness—and felt, for a bitter moment, that he himself was the most futile person alive.

"When did it happen?" he said.

"In April," Dr. Gentian smiled, "At a place called Lexington—and   Concord—near   Boston,   aren't they?   They say the colonials ran like hares."

"You lie," said Andrew, with an intensity that surprised him, "They wouldn't run before a parcel of lobsterbacks."

"No?" said Dr. Gentian. He smiled again. "You will note, Mr. Cave, that our friend has just insulted the entire British army *in toto*."

"I'll note it," said Mr. Cave, greedily, "I'll remember it."

A knock came at the door.

"There, sir," said Mr. Cave, "There are our lobsterbacks now."

He opened the door. Three soldiers headed by a corporal marched into the room and grounded arms. Andrew thought tiredly that they looked like disgruntled footmen in their draggled uniforms. The corporal's face was still puffy with sleep. By some trick of mind he remembered his first tour of inspection when they had passed the tiny guardhouse near the wharves and Dr. Gentian had jested about his military forces. There were only eight men at the post—where were the other five? It seemed inappropriate that they should not join in this nightmare joke of arresting him as a murderer and a rebel.

The corporal was a decent fellow—he had often given him tobacco. But tonight his face was as stiff and wooden as a face carved on the bowl of a pipe. It betrayed not the slightest sign that he had ever seen Andrew before. All soldiers were like that— they came out of a giant toy-box and turned into flat pieces of painted wood whenever someone spoke to them with a frog in his throat. He looked at the corporal's feet accusingly—they should be glued into a little green stand. Also, it was thoughtless of Dr. Gentian to leave his soldiers out in the rain. They would have to be repainted, tomorrow, clumsily, with sticky stuff that came off on your tongue when you licked the brush. Presently he would get up and push the corporal in the chest—then the corporal would totter on his stand and fall in one piece against the nearest private, and all three of them would clatter to the floor with a woodeny sound, because they were only toys, and this was a dream. Dr. Gentian was saying something.

"Put him in the cell with the Minorcan," he was saying. "They are both concerned in the attempt to assassinate Mr. Cave and myself and capture the colony. In addition, this young man is strongly suspected of being in league with the rebellion in the Northern Colonies. Seditious newspapers have been found in his room and his brother is a prime-mover in the revolt. He will be transferred to St. Augustine later, for trial. The charge is treason and attempted murder. Very well, corporal. Take charge of the prisoner."

"Get him up on his feet," said the corporal in a voice of board, "Can he walk? All right—bring him along between you."

They passed by the great main staircase on their

way to the door, and Andrew, turning his head
caught a glimpse of Sparta Gentian. She was stand-
ing half up the stairway, leaning on the rail, the
shawl with the vivid flowers on it wrapped around
her. Their eyes met for an instant. As she looked
at him a slow smile widened on her mouth and her
eyes began to burn. Then she leaned forward de-
liberately and spat at him from the stair.

"Damn the woman—she's spit on my coat,"
grumbled the private on Andrew's right as they went
out of the door.

"Less talk there, you," said the corporal ahead.
"Shut your mouth and pretend you're a duck—it's
raining like bloody hell."

2.

There was darkness and the smell of damp stone
and rotten mold—things ran about in the darkness
on light, innumerable feet. The air was the air of a
cellar that has been built underneath a well. For a
moment Andrew was oddly reminded of the dairy-
house on the country place that bordered the Boston
road—cool even in lion-colored August with the
coolness of slabs of stone buried deep in the ground.
He was a tanned little boy in knee-breeches with
flushed cheeks and damp hair, standing before a
gleaming pan on a table and stretching out a stealthy

finger through the pleasant gloom to dabble its tip in the risen cream, thick and yellow as daffodil-petals clotted together. Through the deep, barred window Summer came and the smell of it, the smell of heat and harvest and grain bursting out of the ear. Then he remembered. The little boy and the cool dairy belonged to another life which some stranger had lived in a void. This was the pit of oppression and he would lie in it like a truss of discarded hay till they took him out to hang him to an orange-tree in the bright morning, while Spanish ladies looked out from behind black fans from the jutting balconies of old houses in St. Augustine, and a curly-haired drummer-boy rattled out a dead march and then, for an instant, silenced his drum.

He moved forward unsteadily, in the darkness. "Sebastian?" he called querulously, "Sebastian?"

There was a stir in a corner.

"I am here, my friend," said a disembodied voice.

"Have they hurt you much, Sebastian?"

"The knife slipped," said the voice in answer. "He was too quick. The knife slipped in my hand." Then it was silent and the running things resumed their activities.

Andrew felt his way over to the corner. His outstretched hand touched a shoulder that winced beneath the touch.

"Have they hurt you much?" he said again.

"No," said Sebastian very bitterly. Andrew's

eyes were growing accustomed to the blackness—now he saw the blur of a face. "I am well enough. But the knife was dedicated—it should not have slipped when I struck."

"I fired at him point-blank," said Andrew sitting down in a puddle. "But the priming was wet. Then they hit me over the head."

"You should have had a silver bullet," said Sebastian. "People like that are not killed with steel or lead."

"I will have a silver bullet next time," said Andrew, and fell silent. The two friends sat together in the dark for some time without saying anything more. Both were gazing into the shadow that encompassed them and Andrew's hand lay lightly on Sebastian's shoulder. There seemed little need of speech between them at the moment—each knew well enough what the other felt and thought. When Andrew had first entered this mildewed night, he had been curious to hear Sebastian's story and eager to tell his own. Now he felt as if both had been told and judged and found unimportant. There were only three things left of any importance, an ache in the skull, a darkness before the eyes, and the quick sound of scuttling feet in the other corners of the room.

After a while, however, Andrew spoke.

"Do you think there'll be a next time, Sebastian?" he said, heavily.

"Who knows?" said Sebastian, "We are always between God's fingers—now no less than ever."

At any other time the words would have struck Andrew as insufferably bigoted and submissive. Now they seemed to him what they were, a calm statement of fact. To Sebastian God was a visible and tangible presence—therefore He was here, in this pit, no more so and no less than He was everywhere. He was with the soldiers in the guardroom, also, as they drank out of empty cups and cut at toy food that stuck to its plate. He was with Dr. Gentian in his study when devils hatched in the fire. No sin could avert that scrutiny, no blasphemy or righteousness deter its penetration by the width of a hair. When the time came for judgment, they should all be judged—meanwhile it behooved them to act according to their lights, for, within their limits of flesh, they were free to do good or evil. God had bound them all with a light, indivisible cord—when He wished, He could gather them up and count them like the buttons on Peggy's button string. In the meantime, He might never lift a finger to avert a present anguish—for so are martyrs left without justification.

Andrew wished that he could think of God like that, but he could not. To him God was something vague to pray to, for happiness or against the approach of pain—something which might be there. God was a cushioned pew and a prayer-book and a

clergyman in robes as opposed to a hard pew and a
long hymn and a preacher in a black Geneva gown.
He had never thought much about God except as a
superior kind of Archbishop of Canterbury who sat
on a cloud and looked at Papists sternly. But
Sebastian was a Papist—and Sebastian had taken
God in his mouth—and God was with him now. It
was very strange and just a little unfair.

"They say I'm a traitor," he said idly, "They say
the Northern colonies have revolted and there was a
fight between our men and the soldiers—and my
brother was in it, so I must be a traitor, too."

"When the ass is spurred too hard it tries to kick
off its rider," said Sebastian, who had proverbs in
his blood, "Are you for the rider or the ass?"

"I don't know," said Andrew, puzzled, "My house
is divided. I should have thought more about it be-
fore. I know my father must be for the King."

"Then you must be for the King," said Sebastian,
with Latin respect for paternal authority, "It is ugly
when a cause divides son and father—even a good
cause."

"I don't know," said Andrew again, "It doesn't
seem real yet." Again he saw the dim picture of his
brother aiming a musket at a toy-soldier corporal—
the picture was fantastic—it could not have occurred.
"I can't believe they're really fighting," he added,
"I can't. The ministry has passed some bad laws,

of course—but Hancock and Adams—who'd ever fight for them?"

"Once men have started to fight, they forget what set them on," Sebastian said, "It is like a game of ball—the ball is nothing—the thing is to throw the ball so it counts for your side. Those who watch the game see better than the players. Only, in war, you cannot stand off and watch the game."

"I don't want to fight the King's soldiers, though," said Andrew, "Why should I? And I certainly can't imagine fighting Lucius."

"You will have to do one or the other," said Sebastian, placidly, "But the winning side is always hard to tell."

"Not this time," said Andrew, feeling his tongue grow curiously bitter, "If there really is a revolt, they'll put it down as they put down the Pretender at Culloden. Butcher Cumberland. They have a trained army. We have nothing. I mean the Colonials have nothing," he added hastily.

"God sometimes gets tired of the man on the ass," said Sebastian, "If I didn't think that, I would strangle myself here with my own hands."

"Perhaps," said Andrew, considering, "But if I were betting, I should bet on the man."

"You have already bet on the ass, my friend," said Sebastian, with a chuckle, "If you had not, you would not be here."

His shoulder was withdrawn from beneath

Andrew's hand. He turned over on his side. "I have some letters from home," muttered Andrew, "I can tell better when I read them—is there ever any light in this place, Sebastian?"

"A little, in the morning. I remember when we first made this cellar, I wondered why it was dug so deep." He was silent. Andrew heard him begin to breathe deeply and quietly.

"What's the matter, Sebastian—are you going to sleep?"

"Why not?" said a drowsy voice, "I may dream my knife did not slip after all."

"I wonder if my head will come off, if I try to sleep," said Andrew to himself. "I suppose it won't, though it feels like it." He stretched himself out on the straw and shut his eyes. "But listen, Sebastian," he said, after a long pause, "Do you really believe God is here in prison with us, in this room?" He waited, but there was no answer. Then he sighed and arranged himself a little more comfortably, hoping the things that ran would not scamper over him much, once he was quiet. In the morning, they could plan, perhaps—not now—the thick stupor of fatigue rocked him in a cradle of lead. It seemed odd that the dawn which would wash the tiny window above him with pale waters of light tomorrow was the very same colored dawn that should have found him dozing in Sparta Gentian's bed, with her hair spread over their pillow like a scarf of drawn gold.

3.

As Sebastian had said, light came to their habitation in the morning—a slanting, shallow column, but enough to enable Andrew to read his letters. Also they had been given fresh water and a dish of boiled rice. The corporal had brought them these, but had refused to answer any questions. Andrew had asked for a razor, which was, of course, denied.

"I never saw them hang a fellow with a beard," the corporal remarked judicially after the request, "But then I haven't seen much hanging." His mouth was sad. "When they hung the great pirates at Execution Dock I was as near to it as could be, but somebody had to stay with Gramfer. Crippled all up he was, and twice he'd fallen in the fire with nobody by. Well, I was the youngest and the least account, so I didn't see it. They say Kidd made a fine show. My father saw him," he added, with some pride. "Twirled he did and kicked for a while. Well, 'tis all in the drop, they say—a proper drop and 'tis over as soon as bite your nails," he concluded cheerfully and disappeared.

Andrew could not hate the man for his graveyard remarks—his face was as honest and foolish as the face of a giant pumpkin. But he felt his neck tenderly for a moment after the fellow had gone.

Now Sebastian was finishing the boiled rice, and he was reading the last of his letters. From them he got anxiety and excitement but little solace. Lexington—Concord—he tried to remember Lexington—he had passed through it once on a memorable trip to Boston with his father and Lucius. He remembered the leathery smell of the coach and how his father had gone to sleep with a red silk handkerchief over his face distinctly enough, but Lexington itself eluded him. A blur of trees—a village green where a goose waddled and stretched out its neck to hiss at a pinafored little girl—a white church with a steeple—the open door of a blacksmith shop where a man in a leather apron spat upon a fiery horseshoe —these scraps were all he could dredge up from the ragbag of memory. He stitched them into a town, in no way different from a dozen other little Massachusetts towns through which their coach had rolled, and yet now, somehow, very different. A month ago, when morning was only half-awake and the shadows lay the wrong way, men had died on that dim grass, awkwardly, unexpectedly—the brimstone smell of burnt powder had drifted in through the windows of the white church and the open door of the smithy— where the goose had waddled the green, bullets had journeyed as casually, with much the same hissing sound. He saw a plump woman with a queer white face stand at the foot of a stairway, listening, and his brother, the macaroni with two watches, dandy no longer but dirty and smooched, with a cut on his cheek, hiding behind a wall to fire at broken red dots running over a bridge. And still he could not comprehend.

"Disperse ye Rebels says He but we were Not for Dispersing . . . So, as I say, We Chast them till they met with their Other Force . . . Lord Percy's it is Said . . . I have a Fine Blister on Both my Feet because of it and a better prospect of Hanging than Ever I had but oh Andrew you should have Seen the Sweet Way they Ran . . ."

That was Lucius' letter. So no more at Present from Yr. Bro. It was odd to think of Lucius, the correct, the mannered, helping Massachusetts bumpkins to hunt a lord like a fox.

One thing, however, stood out plainly. His father was a broken man. Suspected by both sides, the invisible swordsman had forced him to the wall at last. The handwriting in his last epistle was shaky and old—the ends of the letters trailed off feebly as if it had been too great a care to finish them aright. "I have had a Stroke, my dear Sonn, and though they say 'Twas not the True Apoplexy, yr. Mother is greatly Concerned." Andrew felt pain tear at his heart, ragged and sharp. Pain and satire, for the words were followed by a formal blessing "Upon your Projected Marriage." For an instant Andrew wished, humanly enough, that he had never found Sparta out. His father seemed to set such store by the fact that his younger son, at least, was safe from the worries that beset himself. The mood was succeeded by one quite as youthful though more practical. He started up. He must get back to New York at once—see his father—find out the truth of the quarrel between colonies and King. His head was better now and his fever, queerly enough, quite gone. He was almost at the door before he remembered. Then he put his head in his hands and groaned aloud.

He felt Sebastian touch him on the arm. "Come my friend," said a voice, "Sorrow eases the heart, but we have no time for it now. There must be a way out of this hole—the rats come in and go out, and between us we have at least as much sagacity as a rat."

It was later. The slanting column of light through the window had almost disappeared. They had searched the boundaries of their prison, floor and walls, as far as their hands could reach, like misers looking for a penny, and still they had found nothing to aid their escape. Two crannies through which rats could pass, a litter of soiled straw tossed over and over—that was all. Andrew thought of the tools hanging from the bench of the carpenter's shop by the wharf with a hopeless longing. He would have given any dubious immortality for the little file down by the end.

"We must think of some way to get the soldier in

here and knock him on the head," said Sebastian, rising from his knees after a last picking over of the straw. "We cannot take the wall apart with our fingernails."

"Even if we did, though . . ." said Andrew.

"Yes," said Sebastian, "There's only one way out and that's through the guardroom. But it is our only chance."

"Wait a minute," said Andrew. He took up the dish and the pitcher that had held their breakfast and stared at them with greedy searching eyes.

"I thought of that," said Sebastian. He tapped the dish, "Wood," the pitcher, "Clay." "Even if we broke the pitcher, the pieces would crumble on the stone."

"There must be something, somewhere," said Andrew, against reason. Again his eyes slowly traversed the familiar walls of the room from ceiling to floor. Then he stiffened all over like a dog coming to point. High up in the wall and hardly visible in the gloom, beyond the reach of their hands, was a large, projecting nail.

"Get up on my shoulders, Sebastian—there is our tool," he said, his voice shaken as if he had just risen from deep water with a sea-pearl in his hand.

It took an hour or so to work the nail loose from the wall. When they had it down at last, it proved bent and rusty but they gloated over it with a solemn joy.

"Now," said Sebastian, practically, "Where?" and he looked around him.

"We could never tunnel through from below in time," said Andrew. "That stone beneath the window—can you reach it, if you stand on my shoulders again?"

"I can just reach up to the middle of the bar," said Sebastian, after he had tried.

"Sentry outside?"

Sebastian peered cautiously, "I don't see one. But there may be one. There's a ditch, and a little rise beyond it."

"Thank God the light's gone away. He'd hardly see us, anyhow, in the darkness—and we'll just have to chance being heard. Is the window too small?"

"Yes. Even if we could cut the bar."

"Well then," said Andrew, gritting his teeth and wishing Sebastian weighed less. "We'll have to take out the stone."

They spelled each other, all afternoon, at short intervals, the one who was below listening for the footsteps of the guard. The nail grew dull—then sharp again as it filed itself against the stone—then dull once more. Once it almost broke in two and once they were nearly caught by the unexpected return of the corporal soon after he had brought them a scant and nasty dinner. It was hard, exhausting work—the mortar at which they picked was only a little less indurate than the stones it cemented and the man who worked had to support himself with one hand against the wall while his human stepladder suffered rigid agonies in back and loins. When they were too beaten with fatigue to work any more it seemed to them as if they had accomplished as little as a pair of caterpillars gnawing blindly at the sides of an iron box, but at least a beginning had been made. They disguised their work with a paste of mud and spittle and rested achingly.

The next day was the same, and the next—a fever of labor in the dark to the accompaniment of the slight rasp of the worn nail against the stone—a driving of cramped, rebellious muscles to the same monotonous, tiny task. Pick, pick, pick, went the sound of the nail—pick, pick, pick. The sound wore a shallow groove in Andrew's mind. He could hear it continue interminably through the uneasy veil of sleep and his fingers twitched mechanically as if they still held the nail.

Pride and hope alike were gone, the body was gone, of the body only the hands remained, picking, picking unendingly like clumsy thieves at the lock of a closed door. He had long ago ceased to be Andrew Beard. He was a smoke, a shadow, that crawled up upon another shadow's shoulders in obliterated gloom, to pick, pick, pick with a shadowy fang at a deepening crack between two blocks of darkness. Sometimes it was the black, dully-gleaming heart of Night itself at which he dug, and he

half-expected his nail at any moment to slip through
some crack in heaven and shatter itself to bits against
the points of a star.

Why he did what he was doing, he no longer re-
membered. The thought of any actual escape was
buried deep under tiny crumbs of mortar and flakes
of iron-rust. He felt at times that if some one had
opened the door and told him he was free, he would
merely have stared and grunted and returned to the
corner beneath the window to bend his back again
like a burdened ass while Sebastian stood upon it
and nibbled at a coffin of coquina somewhere above
him, for ages, with that slight, rasping sound till his
fingers refused their office and it was time for Andrew
to crawl up and nibble in his turn.

Toward mid-evening of the third day, the stone
could be loosened a little. If both had been able to
get any purchase on it, at the same time, they might
have been able to wrench it away from the bar which
was cemented into it from above. As it was the
stone would only give one useless and exasperating
fraction of an inch, and the problem of the bar re-
mained. The bar, too, was harder to get at, and
they could hardly file it with what was left of the
nail.

"Is it deep sunk, do you think, Sebastian?" said
Andrew, lying dead on the floor after a straining
and unsuccessful attempt to tear the stone out of
the wall by main force.

"I think so," said Sebastian wearily. "We shall have to pick the mortar out of its socket and bend it up somehow. Then, perhaps, the stone will loosen."

"I wish I had your patience," said Andrew, "Myself, I think we shall die before we pick out that mortar."

He rose. "Make me a back, Sebastian. I'll see if I can reach it."

He clung with one hand to the sill and reached the other up awkwardly to pick at the mortar that held the bar. His hand was unsteady with fatigue and the stroke went wild. The nail slipped, his knuckles rapped on the stone. His fingers jerked apart mechanically at the pain, the nail flew out, hopped between the bars and dropped over the outer edge of the window sill. He heard it clink on a stone and felt sick and old. He tried to reach over through the bars, but the window opening was deep and narrow—from his cramped position he could just put his hand out over the outer edge. There was a ditch beyond, a couple of feet in depth, where the nail had fallen. Try as he might he could not reach to the bottom of that ditch.

His muscles gave way. He slid down.

"Kill me, Sebastian," he gasped, "I have lost the nail," and fell in a heap on the floor.

"We must find another nail," said Sebastian, after

a long silence, but even as he spoke both knew that there was no other nail.

"Perhaps, if we rest for a while, we will be able to move the stone without it," said Andrew, but his voice was entirely without hope. The stone had come to have a personality to them both in the hours they had labored upon it. At times they cursed it in hushed voices as one curses an ungrateful woman— at other times they pled with it for a sulky god. Now it had turned into a god forever, a dumb god with a broad, flat, roughened, eyeless face, that sat across the door of life like a plummet of lead, and blocked it, and would not move away.

"We will have to kill the guard after all," said Sebastian, tonelessly. "Kill him somehow and chance to rest." His voice showed the utter desperation of the expedient.

"Stone walls do no-ot a pri-son make. Nor i-ron BARS a c-a-a-g-e—" giggled Andrew suddenly. "That's funny, isn't it, Sebastian? I remember my mother used to sing that—she had a good voice. But the man who wrote the song was a liar all the same. Oh, wasn't he a liar, Sebastian—" he continued, half-hysterically.

"Put me on your shoulders, Andrew," said the other, quietly. "My arm is a little longer than yours —perhaps I can reach it."

Andrew gulped, recovered his wits, and started

to obey. But just as he bent his back, something rattled on the floor.

They looked at each other incredulously, holding their breath—two hunched images of shadow staring at each other intently like apes in a cage. There was another tiny rattle on the floor. Then Andrew felt a pebble strike on his cheek.

"Window, Sebastian," he said fiercely, while hope grew up in his mind like a winter-rose.

It seemed to him that he stood for hours with Sebastian's feet digging into his shoulders while Sebastian whispered hurriedly in Mahonese to another whisper, swift and gentle as the rustle of a green leaf on a budded tree. Then at last Sebastian was down and talking in fierce, little, jerky phrases.

"Caterina," he said, "She managed to get away. There's a sentry but he's a fool. Sleeps. Oh, you English—you think you can watch a rathole with a lazy cat. Boat, by the old wharf. Tomorrow night. They'll think we've gone by land. She'll be at the boat. Your boy helped. Carlos. He says you gave him a dollar. He's very grateful."

"What about the nail?" said Andrew, still tormented by its loss.

"We have better than nails now," said Sebastian, luxuriously. He opened his hand and showed Andrew a thin glass bottle full of yellow liquid. He shook it lovingly. It rattled. "Files," he said huskily. "Two files. And oil to quiet them."

Andrew began to laugh soundlessly—a painful laughter that racked the pit of his stomach. Then he thought of something else, and his laughter stopped.

"What did they do to her?" he said, trembling.

"Caterina? They whipped her, that next morning. That's why she couldn't come before. Even now—" He stretched out his arms. The slow roll of his voice filled the chamber like the beating of an iron heart. "Oh, Christ on the Cross—" he prayed, "Oh, Christ on the Cross—You have given us a way to the air—Give us vengeance too—if only a little—a little—" He broke off. "We must rest for a while," he said more naturally. "Even with the bar cut through we will need all our strength for the stone."

4.

The bar was all but cut through—the cut plastered over and concealed. Then they had to wait. They had rested longer than they had intended before starting the work, sinking down into a black, murmuring bog of sleep as soon as their heads touched the floor, and when the task was nearly done, the air beyond the window had changed, and, behind dark gauzes, yellow dawn began to stir faintly, like a bird still hidden in the egg. After that, they could sleep again for a while, but not as they had slept

before. They were too tense, the bog refused to re-
ceive them, they napped in uneasy snatches like dogs
before a hunt. Andrew, waking a dozen times, each
time glowered up at the window and was angry to
see how slowly the first pale stiletto of light broad-
ened into a yellow sword.

When the corporal brought their breakfast they
were both broad awake and very restless. They tried
to hold him in talk to make the minutes pass but he
was surly and would only mutter in general terms
against sergeants who cheated honest men out of
their pay with dice that had a spell on them.

"By God," he growled, "if both of you weren't
such traitors, I'd change you a bottle of Augustine
rum for the promise of a couple of knucklebones
after you were hanged. They say a hanged man's
knucklebones make wizardy dice, if he's strung up
in the natural course of crime—but being traitors,
yours wouldn't serve most likely—'tis just my luck
—I never played jailer before except on a black
fellow that stole the Governor's wig for a heathen
idol in Jamaica and he was a poor pagan that didn't
leave me as much as a copper ear-ring. I was born
with a caul, too, but I've never had any luck from it.
When I was christened parson opened the book at
the wrong place and started blazing away at the
Burial Service most savagely before a' could be
halted and it's shadowed me ever since. I can feel
the Resurrection and the Life stuck in my throat at

night like a slice of apple—You're lucky to be decently hanged, you are, there's some more grievous and judgmatical death in store for me, and it rises my dinner in me to have to think of it—" So he mourned himself away, leaving them alone with a vast desert of time.

The light grew, the hours dragged, they could not keep their eyes from the bar and the stone. They would talk to each other feverishly for a while and then, without intention, fall suddenly into a staring silence. Andrew found at last that he was talking to himself under breath. "Night," he was murmuring. "Night. Oh *lente, lente, currite, noctes equi*—" no, that was the wrong quotation, that asked night's coursers to slacken their pace.

"What time do you suppose it is, Sebastian?" he said for the twentieth time.

"We must have hours yet," said Sebastian. Andrew had expected the answer, but he sighed all the same. He looked at the bar again. To the eyes of both the crack in it had grown, all through the morning. Now it yawned—a blunt, metal mouth, insecurely stuffed with mud and straw. It seemed impossible that the stupidest of jailers should not detect it at a glance.

"Sebastian, do you think if—" began Andrew, and stopped himself. He must keep his eyes from the bar—if he did not something would make him leap up and swing from it chattering like a monkey. For a moment he half-wished the corporal had seen the crack and suspected. Anything was better than this waiting. Then he made a sort of formless prayer to anything which might be listening not to pay the slightest attention to his wish.

There were footsteps in the corridor—coming nearer. Andrew felt his body grow taut—glancing over at Sebastian he saw that he too was rigid. His wish had been granted. They were found out. They were coming to take them to some other cell, deep down, where even a file would be of no use. They were coming to hang them, now, while the light still held and the air was sweet.

The door opened. The corporal was there with two other men.

"You're wanted," he said, jerking his thumb at Andrew. "No—not you—him," as Sebastian started to rise.

Andrew got up slowly, feeling sweat on his palms. Sebastian and he were to be separated—ironed perhaps. Either step would be fatal to both, now. Why hadn't they chanced it last night?

"Who wants me?" he said, licking his mouth.

"You're wanted," said the corporal, grinning. "Come on now—shake a leg."

"*Adios, amigo*," murmured Andrew stiffly as he passed Sebastian. They touched hands.

"Come on now," said the corporal impatiently,

"Last Wills and Testaments not executed at this shop without longer notice."

5.

"Well, Andrew," said Dr. Gentian, pleasantly, "I am sorry to see you so unkempt. I wish I could lend you a razor. When I was in prison at Poona," he continued reflectively, rubbing his chin, "I managed to shave with a broken cowrie-shell. But it was a painful expedient, at best. I should not advise its imitation, though it passes the time as well as trying to tame a rat. I wonder at the patience of those men who find prison-rats so easy to tame. Mine were savage little beasts—Orpheus himself could not have made them affable." He broke off, tracing a little pattern with his right thumb in the silver scrollwork on the butt of Andrew's pistol.

The two were alone—the soldiers had retired outside the door. Andrew, through lowered lids calculated the distance between them and the possibility of springing across the table and getting that firm throat between his hands before the balanced forefinger could pull the trigger.

"I wouldn't," said the doctor, smiling. "This priming happens to be dry and—let me compliment you on your taste in small-arms, Andrew. You may not have observed it, but this particular pistol is a weapon of delightful precision. I experimented with it this morning upon a humming-bird—the poor thing was blown into feathers at twenty paces."

"What do you want with me?" said Andrew, heavily. His eyes were still blinking with the un-accustomed plenty of daylight in this windowed room. He had almost forgotten there were such rooms, he realized, now—and realized too, distaste-fully, the scarecrow figure he must cut before the Immaculate Doctor. His clothes were ragged and foul—dirty stubble covered his face—he had not been clean for days. His eyes were furtive—his body had a prison smell to it—when he walked, he walked like a prisoner, with a heavy, shuffling step. In a tale, such tiny things would not matter to the heroic captive—it was monstrously unfair that they should matter now.

"I wanted to see you, Andrew," said the Doctor, softly, "and now that I have, I confess myself satis-fied."

Andrew hardly heard him—his mind was busy with a different problem. "For God's sake tell them to give me a clean shirt, you devil!" he burst out suddenly, and instantly felt ashamed.

The Doctor laughed. "Your request is quaintly put," he said, with enjoyment, "but I'll grant it. You shall have a clean shirt—yes, Andrew—and soap and a razor—and go wherever you wish. For a price, of course," he added, tracing his pattern.

Andrew had straightened up at the first of his words. Now his shoulders sagged again.

"There would be," he said, flatly, "No."

"You haven't heard my terms yet," said the Doctor. "I ask very little. Only a lapse of memory." He looked at Andrew but Andrew did not reply.

"I do not even ask you to go on with your projected marriage." He continued, "A son-in-law," his thumb crept along a tiny silver scroll, "whose brother is—disaffected—whose father—will be bankrupt—would hardly fit with my plans. All I ask is—seven days forgotten. Completely. Your word on it. Then you're free."

"Why?" said Andrew, bluntly. "Why not hang me out of hand at once?"

"Oh—call it a whim—a vagary" said the Doctor with masked eyes, "I've always rather loved fools— after my own fashion. And then—I'll be frank enough—trying you in Augustine would be such a tedious business—I could carry it through—don't mistake me—but there might be embarrassing questions. I'd rather have your word."

"Suppose I broke my word?"

"To be frank," said the Doctor, "I do not care very greatly what you do—out of the Floridas. Till then—you would sign a—confession—I have drawn up. You could have it back—in time."

"Confession of what?" said Andrew.

"Oh—not too much," said the Doctor, pursing his lips. "Disloyalty, chiefly—an attempt on my daughter's honor, perhaps—just enough to discredit you. I assure you I should use it with the greatest reluctance," and, strangely enough, Andrew thought that he spoke the truth.

"Sebastian and Caterina?" he said.

The Doctor pondered. "You can have the girl," he said finally. "I should regret it, but after all— Mrs. Gentian deserves consideration. The man, no. I must keep discipline. But I might merely send him to St. Augustine prison, then."

"What happens to him otherwise?" said Andrew, breathing.

"The currycomb," said the Doctor in a wisp of voice. "A distressing end."

Andrew looked at him.

"I should really advise against it," said the Doctor very softly, with his forefinger alert. "You could not possibly reach me in time. Besides, there are always the soldiers."

Andrew drew a long breath.

"And—I—?" he said.

"Oh, you would merely hang," said the Doctor, recovering his cheerfulness. "Merely hang. You're young to hang, Andrew."

Andrew passed his hand over his eyes, trying to think. He could save Sebastian's life, Caterina's, his own. Sebastian was patient and clever—even in the dungeons of St. Augustine he might find some way of escape. Then they would all be saved. The other way was death. He could refuse for himself, and die, but he would not have to die in torment as Sebastian must.

For an instant he saw himself free, at the rail of a ship, with Caterina at his side. Her hand was lightly on his, she was telling him he had done well, her eyes were gentle. Cool as the fronds of lilies floating on a hushed and evening pool, her fingers touched his, and met, and somewhere, Sebastian was smiling at them both from his dungeon . . .

His mind revolted from the mirage, smarting with shame and self-disgust. Dr. Gentian was very adroit. He had put this thing so subtly that he, Andrew, could not only save himself but Caterina for himself and fool his mind into thinking he had acted nobly. No one could accuse him if he did this —Sebastian would not—his own spirit might for a while but it would grow sleepy—a year from now, this present would be forgotten, buried under a drifting red-and-yellow heap of leaf-brittle days like the skeleton of a rat, to crumble into earth and water and sun. And Sebastian would be still in his dungeon—but perhaps Caterina and he could buy him out somehow if he had not died . . .

The stone. The bar. The escape.

But it seemed impossible that they should really escape. Dr. Gentian was too strong. He had been in prison himself—he would not have left them there, together, unchained, without providing against any escape. All the time that they had been gnawing in the dark he had been outside the window, listening, smiling, till he could no longer contain the mirth in his belly and went slowly back to laugh at them aloud with the devils that lived in the chimney of his study. Yes, he must have been doing that.

There was no use trying to bargain with him over Mr. Cave's projected plan of revolt. He knew of that, too, undoubtedly—and if, by some miracle, he did not, it offered the one slim chance that, in the confusion of such an event, they might escape indeed.

Was he overrating Dr. Gentian's powers? Perhaps. But as he stared at him now, with heavy eyes, he saw him as a man no longer, not even a Cæsar, but something inhuman, with the transient powers of the inhuman over human stuff. An undying figure that walked from the East, with a cloud of flies above it, and a gilt pomander in its hand.

"Aren't you ever afraid of hell?" he found himself saying, queerly, with a catch in his voice. "I should think you'd be afraid of hell."

The smile on Dr. Gentian's face became a rictus cut in ivory, the muscles of the jaw stood out.

"Why this is hell, nor am I out of it," he quoted in a slow, dry voice. " 'Think'st thou that I'—did you ever read Marlowe, Andrew? The style is very impure—bombastic, even—he cannot compare with Pope—but there are things in his Faustus which—"

He stopped. His mouth relaxed. But while he spoke, there had been something in his face that Andrew had never expected to see there—a turn of the mouth—a shape behind the eyes—something ruined and very lonely—a statue defaced—a barren bough in the gale.

It passed. "Well?" said the easy voice.

Andrew looked at the floor. He was twenty-two. When you were twenty-two, Death was something far-off that happened to other people. It needn't happen to him for a long time.

What if the Minorcans were oppressed? They weren't actually slaves. They got along. Some people, maybe, had to be oppressed. It wasn't his quarrel.

Then he saw them, young and old, women and children, the dead on the voyage, the dead in the first months of fever, the priest swinging in his robes, the sallow boy, screaming, under the currycomb. But it wasn't his quarrel.

There were two doors open. One meant life, and a clean shirt, and Caterina's hand on his hand, by the rail of a ship, at night, while the moon climbed up in heaven like a silver woman. The other was death for all of them. He shut his eyes and chose death.

"No, I won't," he said, in a voice he was surprised to find so even.

Dr. Gentian sighed. "I'm sorry," he said. "Dying is so wasteful. You can have twenty-four hours to think it over, Andrew. I will see you again tomorrow, when they are up. Think it over. Sergeant," he called and struck on a bell. "I hate to hang you, Andrew—it will be a great nuisance. I had a parrot once that amused me. I had to wring its neck. It is much the same. You may take the prisoner back now, Sergeant, if you will."

6.

"He gave me twenty-four hours," Andrew ended. He looked at his friend.

"It is more than enough," said Sebastian. "We shall escape in twelve."

Before the certitude of his tone the image of Dr. Gentian that towered in Andrew's mind like a genie rising from a bottle in a blue, magic fume, diminished gradually. He became what he was, a man of great parts, whose knowledge of his own abilities had swollen with power till it festered, and so spoiled a tyrant instead of making a king. Seen so, he was no longer terrific or even hateful, only beggared, as all men are beggared in one way or another who seek from life a passion more intense than the body can bear. He was a king in check—a torch inverted—a fire that wasted itself against a column of salt—and as Andrew began to perceive this, slowly and delicately as the slow lifting of a slab of bronze from his breast, the fear of death passed from him and left him composed. It would return, undoubtedly, but for this moment, brief as the flight of a bird between tree and tree, it had gone. He could smell the mignonette in his mother's garden. Dr. Gentian could kill them both, but that was all he could do.

"What are you going to do, Sebastian, when we are free?" he said casually, out of a strange peace.

"Tell the governor to free my people," said Sebastian. The cool stone of peace had touched at his lips as well, he spoke with the simplicity of a ghost. "When they are free—" he shrugged. "Who knows? Life is long—there are many things to do before the priest comes with his oil. If I had money I should like to buy a fishing-boat—my father was a fisherman. I should like to marry, too, and have a son. It is good to have a son to help you draw in the nets. And you, my friend?"

"I shall go North," said Andrew. "Perhaps to help the ass you spoke of kick off his rider—yes." It was the first time he had definitely put the thought at the back of his mind into words. He was astonished to find how rational it sounded. "After all— as long as they've called me a traitor—" he said, musingly. He wondered if that were really what he would do. It was difficult to see himself with a ragamuffin musket, presenting it at Lion and Unicorn.

Sebastian nodded. "I thought so," he said. "There are three things one cannot run away from —war, love and death." His voice held that indolent fatalism that has so often deceived the North by its languid pride. "Sometime I should like to go back to Minorca," he confessed. His eyes glittered. "This is a good country, here, but it is not Fererias."

"Tell me about your island," said Andrew, childishly. He settled himself in a corner to listen.

"You'd laugh at it, if you went there," said Sebastian. "It is small and harsh and poor. But the people are friendly there. My uncle lives in Mahon, if he has not died—he is a very friendly and hospitable person. My aunt has copper pans in her kitchen," he continued, with some pride. "They tease her about being rich—she is not—they came from her father who was a copper-smith—but few of us have copper vessels, even in the town—" His voice droned on, lulling Andrew into the content of a sleepy child. It was now almost entirely dark in their cell, though outside the sun had not yet set. There would be hours still before they would be safe in cutting through the rest of the bar, but now Andrew did not care how many there were. The fear of death no longer ran about with the rats in the darkness and he was quite happy listening to the slow story of certain doings in the family of a foreign copper-smith which could not possibly interest any person of gentility.

7.

Dr. Gentian laid his book down with a sigh, and glanced at his watch. He rose, and stood for a moment, observing how surely and skilfully the petal of a flower grew in rose-colored silk upon gauze, under the deft, shining strokes of his wife's embroidery needle.

"That must tire your eyes, my dear—especially at night," he said, with solicitude.

"I am never tired." She did not turn her head to answer. "Are you going now?"

"Yes, my dear. I am going now. You need not wait up for me. I shall not be back till late."

She made a knot in the silk. "You never believe me," she said. "Even if I told you, you were walking into a pitfall—you wouldn't believe me."

He smiled, "I should merely think your natural concern for my safety had overbalanced your excellent reason," he said.

"No doubt," she said wearily, her face still averted. "Well—you can go, then. I shan't wait up."

"It matters to you still," he said, consideringly. "That seems strange."

"Strange enough." Her eyes were fixed on her work. "You'd be a clever man, Hilary, if you left well enough alone."

"A clever man never leaves well enough alone," he said and smiled.

The silk thread broke in her fingers. "You're blind," she said. "Blind and deaf. There's a shadow on your back tonight. But you're deaf and blind. You only think of playing cat and mouse with that boy."

"One must have games." The Doctor's tone was amused. "And cat and mouse is an excellent game, for the cat."

"You'd better watch your daughter." She turned her face now and looked at him.

"My dear!"

"I've told you. She and her lackey. They've been too quiet these last days. Oh, well—go your road. But my Greeks talk to me. There's a rat in the wall of this house, Hilary—a rat in the wall—"

Her voice ceased. Her fingers busied themselves re-threading the needle.

"I think you have the gift, tonight," he said quietly, regarding her. "See for me, my dear."

His hand fell on her shoulder, light as a butterfly. She put it off. "No," she said in a dry, thin voice.

"You're wrong. I haven't had the sight for years. If I had it tonight, would I use it? No."

"Not for me?" His mouth had honey in it.

"No." Her fingers were moving again, she seemed to have no mind for anything but her silk. "Not for you."

He sighed. "Be consoled," he said. "I shan't live for ever. Indeed, sometimes I wonder that I have been able to live this long."

"It would be like you to die first," she agreed, remorselessly. A flash passed over her face. "I'd save you from that," she said, with a prick of her needle.

He chuckled a little. "I believe you. I believe you, indeed. But if something should—cripple me, for instance—just enough—eh?"

She drew in a deep breath. "Some time," she said, huskily. "Soon or late. The candle's not burnt to the wick yet. I can wait for it."

"Really, sometimes, one would think you believed in the fates, my dear. If one didn't know you."

"I believe in waiting," she said, nodding her head. "Yes, I believe in waiting."

His fingers twitched, momentarily. "I wish you'd see for me," he said.

She made no reply. He hesitated for a moment, oddly indecisive. Then he looked at his watch again and turned toward the door.

"Good night, my dear."

The second petal of the flower was half-completed,

the needle stitched on, the face was averted anew. "Good night," said the dry, colorless voice. Dr. Gentian passed out of the room. With his hand on the latch of the front door he hesitated for a second time and threw a glance back up the stairs. Then he shook his head impatiently, opened the door and went out.

As soon as his footsteps had died away, Mrs. Gentian rose. Very softly indeed, she climbed the stairs to the upper corridor and paused, listening, outside the door of her daughter's room. She scratched on the panel twice, gently—no sound replied. "Sparta," she called in a low, sharp voice, waited, repeated the call. The name fell into darkness and was absorbed, no echo mocked it even. Mrs. Gentian laughed under her breath and opened the door of the room. The light of her candle showed it empty, the bed undisturbed. She nodded, as if in assent to an unspoken query and stood in the doorway for a moment, erect as an effigy, not seeming to notice that when her candle guttered it shook flecks of hot wax on her dress. Then she shut the door and went softly down the stairs again, returning to her chair and her needlework. Her face seemed at once resolved and satisfied, and, for a time, the pattern of her embroidery had never grown more swiftly. Then, after a while, the pace of her fingers slackened and stopped. The embroidery still lay in her lap, but she worked at it no longer, though she remained sitting in the chair, with folded hands and that curious expression on her face, her head bent a little forward, as if she were listening for the wind to bring her a piece of long-expected news.

Meanwhile, Dr. Gentian was walking briskly down the road to the guardhouse. He carried a light cane in one hand and was humming to himself and now and then cutting little flourishes in the air with his cane. The moon was up enough for him to pick his way along the well known path without hesitation, while his mind turned over one thing and another in its usual active fashion. His wife's words had stirred him more than he cared to admit and, not for the first time, he felt, with some annoyance, that there was some quality in her which even he could only master by snatches, unless she willed to have it so.

She was the only person he had ever met who did not sooner or later betray himself or herself by talking too much. He had taught her that trick of reticence, likely enough—but now it seemed to him, uneasily, that the pupil was beginning to outstrip her master. It must not be so—yet what could he do to change it? He could not deal with her as he dealt with others—from their first meeting he had thought of her as the living symbol of his luck and the broadening of that vein of superstition which was his weakness, during these later years, had only increased the feeling. The fierce passion that had first united them was long extinguished, but her words still carried a certain weight of omen for him, and at times he came closer being afraid of her than he ever had been of any merely human being.

He smiled a little, recalling certain events. What a sharp, wild, dazzling creature she had been in her first youth—not fair in Sparta's fashion, not fair at all in the way he consciously admired, but with a fire in her like the fire at the heart of his emerald. Wooing her had been like wooing a tiger-cub—his mind still bore the scars of it, for all its balance, as his body bore the thin, seamed scar of the knife she had struck him with, long ago, when she thought he looked too often at that dark little Cypriote. For an instant his body felt young, and he saw, from a tossing boat, a torch flaring at the mouth of a cave and a girl's intense and eager face in the red gush of light.

She would not strike him with a knife again. That had been in the days of their passion, and they and his youth were over. Her love had taken a deal of killing, certainly. He felt that to be unfortunate, honestly enough, for unnecessary ugliness always offended him. But it would have been the same with any other man—she was not the sort that lived easily. In any event, she hated him now, but it did not matter, for, in spite of her hate, he had a unique sort of confidence in her. The struggle between them would only end with life, but in the pauses of it they understood each other.

He smiled—it would seem a queer way of living to that boy in the guardhouse. One had to give up youth to taste the full flavor of hazard—youth lacked the steadiness of hand. For himself, the constant experiment of sharing meat and drink, year-in, year-out, with a creature whose heart still held the savage so barely kept in check by mere adroitness of eye and hand, was life and a good one. Some day, no doubt, the eye would fail or the hand lose cunning, and he would be torn. Well, let it be so, he had had his game.

Meanwhile, there were other diversions, such as that he purposed for this evening. He would think of that now, and taste it in expectation. But when he tried to do so, his wife's words beat in his ears, and he came to a halt for a moment, leaning a little on his cane. After all, it was possible to alter his plans. He had given too much time to young Beard these last months—too little to the plantation. Cave, too, he had been careless recently with Cave— he suspected Cave and the lesser animals in general of getting a little out of hand. Perhaps it might be well to—then he shook his head. His project for to-night was too well matured—tomorrow would be time enough for Cave and the others. He cut a weed down with his cane and went on, but, though a stranger would have thought his bearing composed enough, he was not entirely at ease.

Now it seemed to him that he could hear movement far off in the woods at his left. He stopped again and listened. Something was abroad in the woods, undoubtedly, but the sound was too indistinct for him to make it out clearly. A shadow darted between two trees near the road—a man with a bag on his back—he opened his mouth to call at it—no, it was only a trick of the eye. As for the distant sound, now quieted, it might be a couple of strayed deer or a band of half-tame Indians on a rice-stealing expedition—the latter most probably. The Indians had been growing bold, lately—he must see to that, too. Again, he was almost on the point of turning back to the coquina-house. Then he looked at his watch once more—it was later than he had supposed—the tiny fact decided him. He marched on, swinging his cane—the moon had a bright face tonight—the features of the man in it were distinct. He thought of the old story and smiled. The moon, as a post of observation, would have its advantages.

He turned a corner—there were guardhouse and storehouses below him, their roofs wintry with moonlight. The quiet familiarity of the scene blew the last of his uneasiness away—he had never felt more sure of himself or his luck. A few paces away from the guardhouse door he was challenged in a low voice by a sentry, held a conversation in whispers for a minute, and then went in.

The minutes passed, the still, glittering face rose higher in the sky till the night was perfect. It cast a long straggling shadow over the barred window of Andrew's cell and a bright pool on the floor of Sparta Gentian's empty chamber. In the deep woods that gave upon the St. Augustine road it barely pierced enough to touch with occasional silver the faces and bodies of men and women who came slipping silently between the trees, one by one, like deer trooping together, till the road was full of them. They came from the direction of the colony, burdened with packs or children—there seemed no end to their number—they greeted each other in hushed voices—soon the first of them were filtering away down the road.

In the colony itself the silver dagger fell upon a different sort of surreptitious stir, and a clotting together of shadowy shapes on the skirts of the Italian quarter. Dr. Gentian had wished better than he knew when he had wished for a post of observation upon the cold peaks of the moon, and it was unfortunate for him that his wish could not have been granted. As it was he sat in the guardhouse, tapping his snuffbox and recapitulating the heads of a certain discourse he intended to deliver shortly, ignorant that events already in train were to render that discourse quite unnecessary.

Mrs. Gentian, however, was soon to be better informed. Her rigid attitude of the listener had not altered for the last half hour, she sat in her chair like a sculpture, her hands were marble. Only her eyes discovered life in them, deep in the pupils, contained, patient and somehow dreadful in its certitude, like the life in the eyes of a spirit caught in a cleft stone. She was waiting for a sound, and already the last moments of her vigil were upon her. A mile away, even as one shape among the clotted shapes at the edge of the Italian huts began to issue orders to the others, a Greek boy watched from a shadow and then crawled off, to break into a run for the coquina-house as soon as he was well away from the huts.

PART FOUR: *The Fire on the Beach*

PART FOUR:

The Fire on the Beach

The file grated for an instant and then bit air. Andrew gave a tug at the bar and nearly fell over backward as it came out in his hand. He stared at it incredulously. The end of their work had come.

"We're through, Sebastian," he whispered, "Sebastian, Sebastian, give me a hand with the stone!"

The stone was stubborn, but at last they managed to pry it free. Then they stood and gazed at the gap for a second of triumph.

It only lasted a second. Even while they gazed at it they knew, dreadfully, that they had miscalculated. The hole was just too small. Both tried it, hopefully, defiantly, hopelessly.

"Cut through another bar," said Andrew, finally, when they knew they were beaten, "Cut through another bar." The thought of starting in at the beginning again appalled him so that he could not trust himself to say any more. This last stroke, at the very edge of deliverance, was the worst of all. He had thought himself free of Fear—he had been a child shaking a rattle. Fear had only crept away for a moment to make its return more deadly—now it

settled into his back like a huge, soft animal whose
claws were iron needles. He could feel the cold, salt
sweat of it on his forehead and hands.

"Anyhow, it will give us two weapons instead of
one," muttered Sebastian with bitter philosophy as
he worked in a contained fury of haste. Andrew
could have hated him for saying that, if there had
been time. But there was no time for either hate or
thought or self-pity—there was only time for fear
and the continuous, muffled grate of the file.

After a while they discovered that, with the stone
gone, they could cramp themselves against each
other perilously in such a way that both could file.
Even so, it took an eternity till the second bar was
cut through. But at last that too was accomplished.

"Now," said Sebastian, shivering. "Now, my
friend."

Half the window was blocked by his shoulders—
then he was worming out on his side. Andrew's last
view of him was of a pair of shoe-soles that waggled
absurdly for a moment and disappeared. He waited
ten breaths. No sound. Sebastian must be safe in
the ditch. He transferred the iron thing he was
clutching to his left hand. It was cold in his hand.
He gulped and started to follow Sebastian.

He slid into the ditch head-first, and lay there on
his belly, flat as a lizard. After his days of confine-
ment the outside world seemed formidably large and
open. He was glad for the walls of the ditch—even

with their protection, he felt as lonely and conspicuous as a shelled oyster. He listened. All that he could hear was the distant bubble of water in an irrigation canal and the mutter of wind in the palms. Now the wind rattled a dry leaf somewhere, like a boy shaking a fan, and he started. Where was Sebastian? He stretched out his hand, by inches, and was enormously relieved when at last it touched a shod heel.

"Sebas—" he started to whisper.

"Ssh," a whisper answered "Sentry." The heel started to writhe away from him. He followed it, doing his best to make no noise. That had been the plan, to worm along the ditch till they were on the side of the prison farthest from the guard-room, opposite the smaller storehouse. Then they would have to take to the open.

This crawling was a slow, ludicrous business, especially when you had to carry a bar of iron in one hand. For a moment he was reminded of a sack-race, and almost giggled aloud. How the devil did Sebastian get ahead so fast? He could get along faster if he dropped this silly bar. No, better not.

They were around the corner now. He raised his head, gingerly, and caught a glimpse of the black bulk of the storehouse. Sebastian had stopped. A hand came back through the darkness and dug into his shoulder. Keep quiet, that meant. He lay frozen to the ground.

Suddenly, and without the slightest warning, a grumbling voice spoke out of invisibility—a voice that seemed not a dozen feet away from his head.

"Devil fly away with this musket—my arm's gone asleep again!" it said, in tones of cockney irritation. Something stamped on the ground.

"Shut your mouth, you misbegotten son of a sweep," said another voice, low and irate, "Are you a soldier or a nursemaid?"

"I'm a nursemaid," grumbled the first voice— Andrew knew it now—it belonged to one of the privates who had marched him to prison—the other voice was the sergeant's. "A bloody private nursemaid to a couple of stinkin' prisoners what's going to escape and what never escapes. Why in 'ell can't 'Is Majesty let 'em escape in daylight wen a man can see to shoot?"

"You let them get through and you'll find out what, soon enough," said the other voice, grimly. "Orders are, take alive or dead. Remember that."

"Just button 'em up in my pocket *I* suppose," said the first voice in an unimpressed whine. The other voice seemed to choke for a while. When it recovered it discussed a question of ancestry with some vividness.

"Oh, all right, sergeant, all right," commented the first voice, resignedly. "But a man can't 'elp 'is feelin's. If it was an eskylade now, I'd be breathin' as easy as a babby. But this 'ole and corner work

ain't work for a soldier. W'y can't 'Is Majesty
shoot the pore buggers 'imself if 'e wants 'em shot?
Tell me that, now," it concluded triumphantly,
"an' I'll stand you a pot o' beer."

"Go ask him," said the sergeant's voice, very
bitterly, "Go ask him, Bowbells. He's in the guard-
room now, just waiting for some son of a whore to
ask him a question like that. By God, he'd crucify
you."

"Like enough," grunted the other. "Doctor 'e
calls 'imself." He spat. "*I* wouldn't trust him to
poison a sergeant."

"You're a drunk disgrace to the British Army,"
said the sergeant's voice with sour finality, "And
I'd have you in the calabooze this minute if—"

"Aye," said the other, thoughtfully, "*If* I wasn't
a pearl o' marksmen—and if you could draw a
cordon round 'ere without me—and *hif* I didn't
know 'oo buggered the last payroll—Most likely.
Run along, sergeant, and wipe the other boys' noses
for 'em. You can rest easy about this side—there'll
be two beautiful corpses to show 'Is Majesty if they
tries to run *my* post."

"You're drunk, you fool," said the sergeant
acridly, and departed. "Wish I was," said the other
voice, a trifle plaintively, as Andrew heard the
heavy boots crunch away.

He raised his head cautiously, inch by inch.

There was a little bush at the lip of the ditch—it would hide him as he reconnoitered.

The sentry was just too far away, in the shadowed door of the storehouse. For all his sleepy arm, he seemed terribly alert and there were at least thirty yards of open moonlit ground between him and them. If they rushed him, one of them would be killed or disabled in the rush and the other would have to kill at once, in his turn, before the shot brought up the rest of the guard.

It was like Dr. Gentian, this. Very like him. He could see Dr. Gentian in a cane-chair in the guard-room, waiting composedly for his birds to fly into the snare.

He sank back into the ditch again. He felt stiff and cramped. Dying couldn't be much worse. Sebastian had turned around somehow, he could see his face. He put his own face close. "When you say, Sebastian," his lips formed, without sound. He saw Sebastian's body grow taut and his own muscles tightened. Then Sebastian's expression changed. "Not yet," he whispered. He hunched down and began to crawl still farther along the ditch.

Andrew followed him without hope. As he crawled, he thought of a rat he had seen once in a stable. It was an old, sick-looking rat with grey streaks in its fur and it had been hitching slowly along the wall, looking for its hole. When it had heard his step it had shown yellow teeth in a weak snarl and crouched to the floor and he had realized that its eyes were white and blind. He felt a certain kinship now for that rat.

They had reached the end of the ditch on that side of the guardhouse. Sebastian had stopped and was raising himself up a little. Madness. No, not entirely. The ground fell away sharply beyond this part of the ditch. If they could take five steps across a swathe of moonlight they could roll into a shadow. But even as Andrew saw this, the sentry at the storehouse turned his head slowly toward them. He ducked his head down again with a little gulp. If a cloud would only cross the moon! But there seemed to be no real clouds in all the expanse of heaven— only a few little wisps of silver wool that would hardly veil the bright face for more than an instant.

Sebastian was fumbling in the bottom of the ditch for something—a stone. He crouched with the stone in his hand, looking up at the sky. One of the little wisps was blowing toward the moon like a drifted feather. Sebastian drew his arm back, waiting. Now the feather touched the disk, and, for an instant, as Sebastian's stone, cleanly flung, crashed into the bushes at the sentry's left, the heart went out of the moonlight.

The next moment they were out of the ditch and huddled together in the shadow. Andrew, out of the tail of his eye, had somehow caught a glimpse of the sentry whirling away from them to face the

bushes where the stone had fallen. Now every
moment 'he waited for a cry or a musket shot, but
moment after moment passed, and there was neither
shot nor cry. Luck was with them—so far, they
had not been seen. He wondered 'where the other
sentries were posted.

They crawled along to the edge of their shadow,
hugging it fondly. The slight fall 'in ground deep-
ened to a little gully that hid them better—now the
storehouse was between them and the first sentry
and they could breathe a trifle easier. They 'were
going in the opposite direction from the wharves,
but that they could not help till they were sure of
having passed beyond the cordon. ' When it seemed
that they must have done so, they began to circle
back, Sebastian leading the way. He slipped along
like an Indian, Andrew tried despairingly to copy
his lightness of foot. At last they were down be-
low the storehouse and the way ahead seemed clear.
Andrew snatched a look at the sentry through a
screen of brush. The man was yawning, eyes
squinted, head thrown back. He had a ridiculous
impulse to flip a pebble at the gaping mouth, and
between that and dreading the sound of his own
feet was so absorbed that when Sebastian, creeping
ahead of him, suddenly darted into the door of a
deserted and roofless hut by the side of the wood-
path, his nerves jerked like plucked fiddlestrings.

Once inside the hut, he soon knew the reason for

their taking cover.   There were footsteps and a
mumble of talk coming up toward the hut from the
lower road.   "Tricked," said a leaden accent,
"Tricked, by God.   A pack of lousy indigo-diggers
to trick us so."   Andrew recognized the dull, de-
tested voice with a pang of hate.   A lucid whisper
—serene pulse of gold trembling in hollow of
crystal shell—answered the voice and soothed it.
"It does not matter, Charles.   We can do without
the Mahonese."

"Aye," said Cave.   "Aye.   We'll have to do
without them, now.   But—tricked, by God.   I can't
get over it, sweetheart.   Who'd have thought they
had the guts in them to run away?"

"Charles, Charles, don't think of that now.   We
are wasting time."

There was a mutter, then the voices sank.   Andrew
glared cautiously through a chink in the rotten wall
of the hut.   It was folly he knew, but he could not
lie there and listen without trying to see.   Not ten
steps away, in a patch of moonlight, stood Sparta
and Mr. Cave.   They were talking together in soft,
tense voices—she had her hand on his wrist, she was
wheedling him as if he were an unruly child.

She was dressed entirely in dark stuffs, a dark
handkerchief hid her hair, the cold chastity of the
light gave her features a new beauty, severe, un-
tainted by color, the sharp beauty of the cutting
edge.   Andrew thought of a silver axe in a scabbard

of black glass—she had put away gold for the time and with it the burning gleam of dayspring and planet—the dark handkerchief capped her head as smoothly and reticently as a helmet—she looked like the merciless genius of combat itself, neither man nor woman nor spirit, but something arisen out of the ground with an arrow in its hand. He could see her standing in a chariot, Hippolyta, the amazon queen with the maimed and iron breast, wrapped in the glittering fleece of a golden ram and urging her cloud-born horses like harnessed gods across the tarnished bodies of the dead. For an instant, as her face sank into his mind, it seemed just that it should be so, and he forgot alike that he had loved her and that she had betrayed him.

She had too much of her father in her to live securely, with an even heart. Only violence and the brittle loadstone of danger could release from its cage of sleep, the immortal enemy which lay enchained in that flesh like an archangel in bonds. Now he saw it released, a pillar of darkness, and trembled, but not wholly with fear or hate. The beauty it had was the beauty of the tiger and the killing frost, but it was beauty, and somewhere at a point beyond the system of the stars, the unappeasable ecstasy of its pain lay down on a glittering field and slept between a dove and a hooded eagle. Cave was a different matter—his darkness was the muddy darkness of a fire of wet straw—and Andrew felt he could have killed him without the slightest compunction. But in Sparta, as she was tonight, there was something that would have turned his hand aside.

Now the two separated, having come to some decision between them that Andrew was unable to catch, and Sparta glided away toward the rear of the storehouse. Andrew could only follow her progress vaguely, but it seemed to him that she left a stir in the darkness behind her as she passed. Cave remained where he was for some moments, biting his nails. Andrew gestured to Sebastian, inquiringly —attack him? Sebastian shook his head violently, jerked a thumb toward the way that Sparta had gone and made motions of counting a troop of men. Andrew nodded, his heart thumping. There were others, then—they had blundered into the hut just in time.

He regarded Mr. Cave's back with sullen distaste —would he never move away and set them free? Now he turned, his eye fell casually on the hut, he made as if to come closer but thought better of it. Andrew felt the muscles of his belly contract, and his fingers clench on the bar. A mocking-bird whistled from somewhere, and Mr. Cave grew still. It whistled again and he put his shoulders back and started to walk toward the sentry, crackling the twigs underfoot deliberately as he went as if he wanted the sentry to hear.

The sentry heard and stiffened, musket to his shoulder. "Who goes there?" he challenged softly.

Mr. Cave stopped just on the edge of the open ground. "Overseer Cave," he said in a flat voice, his bearish shoulders stooped.

"Come out where I can look at you, overseer," said the sentry briskly, his eye along the barrel.

Mr. Cave approached slowly. "It's all right, Jenkin," he said in a confidential voice, "I know your orders. They don't apply to me. I've a message for the Doctor."

"Sorry, overseer," said the sentry, lowering his musket, "Have to wait till the sergeant makes rounds again. Strict orders—nobody to pass."

"You can read, I suppose," said Mr. Cave with heavy sarcasm, coming nearer, "I have a pass. Dr. Gentian's signature."

The sentry shook his head.

"Don't know anything about passes," he said. "Show it to the sergeant," but he brought his musket down and leaned forward as if to inspect a paper.

"But I'm in a hurry, I tell you," said Mr. Cave, very near him. Then, to Andrew's astonishment, the sentry continued to lean forward till he had passed his center of balance and, with a gasp, was falling as if he intended to embrace Mr. Cave in his outstretched arms. Mr. Cave caught him deftly and lowered him to the ground.

"Well done, lass," he said in a whisper to the

skirted shadow that had crept around the other
corner of the storehouse and struck the sentry down
from behind. He raised his voice a little. "Come
on, boys," he called softly, and the night was sud-
denly populous with catlike shapes. One stooped
over the fallen sentry—his hand glittered with some-
thing thin and bright—there was the *chuck* of a flat
stone striking water on its edge, and a horrible,
muffled coughing.

"Sergeant of the Guard!" came a doleful howl
from another quarter of the compass, "Sergeant of
the Guard!" A musket shot clanged on the moon-
light. Then events began to succeed each other far
too rapidly for Andrew to keep track of them.

He was out of the hut, with Sebastian, and run-
ning. A man with big white teeth which glittered
like dominoes, rose out of a bush like an evil fairy
and struck at him violently with a long, curved hook.
He felt the iron bar in his hand whirl down and
hit something that smashed like a loaded egg and
jarred his wrist. He stumbled and fell. There
was shouting in his ears and a pop-pop-pop of musk-
etry abruptly silenced. He caught a glimpse of
their lugubrious jailer-corporal jabbing furiously
at something behind a tree. Mr. Cave bellowed a
command—an even voice that Andrew knew called
orders in reply. Something that hummed like a wasp
snipped a twig from a bough in front of his face—
he jerked and went into an irrigation ditch with

a smacking splash—behind him somebody was
screaming "Oh, Jesus, oh, Jesus, oh, Jesus!" in a
high, affronted whine—now Sebastian was pulling
him out of the ditch and they were running again.
Then, abruptly, he was dragged into a dark pocket
between two buildings while a dozen men whose
leader carried a truss of blazing straw on a pole
went by at a trot.

"Where are we?" he wheezed, lungs laboring.
He discovered, with surprise, that the iron bar was
still in his hand. The other end of it dripped.

"They've missed us," said Sebastian. "Too
busy—up there—" He too was panting, but furi-
ously busy, ramming home a charge in a musket
he had somehow acquired.

"Where did"—began Andrew, staring at it,
dazedly.

"Fool with a cap," panted Sebastian. It seemed
sufficient explanation. "Look," he said, "Fire."

Andrew peeped around the corner of the build-
ing. They were still much nearer the guardhouse
than he had supposed. On one hand the moon lit
the scene with precise, bleak radiance, on the other,
a little hut, to the right of the guardhouse, was
burning like a spill of paper with fierce, brief flame.

Mr. Cave and his men had taken such cover as
storehouse and trees afforded. He could see them
swarming in the shadows like uneasy flies. On the
lit and open ground between them and the guard-

house lay a number of broken dolls in attitudes of discomfort. One had on a red coat and lifted up an arm now, to let it drop again as if it were too heavy. There were various cries.

Andrew caught his breath. Dr. Gentian could not have more than a couple of men with him in the guardhouse now. Mr. Cave must have fifty at least. Yet Mr. Cave and his men had not been able to cross that little stretch of open, moonlit ground. True, the besieged were poorly armed and the besiegers had every advantage of shelter, but even so. . . .

Even as he watched, a dozen men dashed out from cover, their heads down as if they were running into a rain, and made for the guardhouse door. They carried a log among them—the intent was evident. A loophole coughed at them and the leading man stumbled and fell as if something invisible had struck him across the shins. The charge wavered— a second man sank slowly to his knees, like a tired horse—the others broke, dropping the log—one of them was wringing his hand and putting it to his mouth, like a boy with burnt fingers. Mr. Cave was cursing.

Something tugged at Andrew's sleeve. "Give me one of your buttons," said Sebastian's voice in his ear, fierce and hurried. "They are silver, aren't they—I must have silver, too—no, a little one—"

Andrew wrenched one of the tarnished buttons

loose from his coat and saw, uncomprehendingly, Sebastian take it, drop it into the narrow, black well of the musket-barrel, ram it down. Then Sebastian was crouching on one knee, muttering to himself, musket poised.

Mr. Cave was roaring in the trees like a bull, trying to lift his men across that patch of open ground. But they would not be lifted, they stuck where they were. There was a weight on their limbs, the invisible weight of a name, it pressed them to the earth. The beasts had turned on the beast-tamer, but they were still afraid of his whip.

Andrew caught a second's glimpse of Mr. Cave, as he darted from one shadow to another, raging. Sebastian cursed softly—the glimpse had been too short for him to fire. Now they heard a shrill, frightened squealing, and the thud of boots kicking flesh. Mr. Cave encouraging his followers. Then again, for an instant, he was in clear view, recklessly exposed against the glare of the burning hut. His hands were cupped to his mouth, he was calling aloud.

"Come out, you damned old wizard!" he roared, in a furious, weeping voice, "Come out and surrender—your life if you'll surrender!—if you don't, by God, we'll roast you there in your shell!"

A flash answered from a window and Mr. Cave's broad hat spun from his head as if a gust of wind had tweaked it. Dr. Gentian's clear, sharp voice called back something in Italian, threat or promise, and Andrew could see the besiegers stir uneasily in the darkness. Then four things happened, almost in the same instant.

A man with a bloody face and a naked scythe in his hand burst out of a clump of darkness, followed by a score of others, and fell upon the flank of Mr. Cave's forces. The clear, sharp voice cried out to them like a joyous cock. Mr. Cave, his body convulsed, leapt to rally his men—and the musket in Sebastian's hands exploded.

It was a long shot, and at first Andrew thought that it had missed. Then he saw Mr. Cave hitch, queerly, in his stride, get on again, and then collapse slowly into the ground, as if quicksand had taken him. A form that must have been Sparta's, for it had streaming hair, ran out of an eddy of conflict and fell upon the body like a dog on a grave.

"The wharves!" called the clear, sharp voice, weaker now, but still very joyous. "Head them off from the wharves, you Greeks—they're making for the wharves!"

They were running again. There was clamor and a flare behind them, where men hunted other men in the moon-splashed darkness like terriers chasing rats in a moonlit barn. Sebastian was ahead of him—behind there were many, but the beaten Italians were throwing their weapons away and calling

"Surrender—Surrender—" in high, shrill voices. Andrew threw a glance over his shoulder, and saw, in a nightmare flicker, a fellow twenty yards behind him stare stupidly at a point of steel that stuck abruptly out of his breast and fall, tripping the man who had run him through the back. Then the ground under Andrew's feet rang hollow suddenly —the wharf. He slipped on greasy wood—was down on his knees—up again. "Here" called Caterina's voice—he caught at a hand—leapt— sprawled into the bottom of a rocking boat.

There was an oar somewhere—he grabbed at it and began to splash with it furiously. They were moving away from the wharf now, but the damn sail wouldn't catch the wind. *Row!* The boat seemed to stick in the water like a bug in a stream of molasses but the gap between it and the wharf was widening—just in time, for there was shouting behind them now. He stole a glance back. There was the man with the bloody face. His left arm dangled at his side like a broken stick. He was yelling something and pointing. There was a ragged spatter of sound—something jumped under Andrew's oar like a frog taking water—he heard a gasp from the bow of the boat. "Hit, Caterina?" he called, but "No, no," said a voice.

Then the sail filled at last, and the wind and the current took them. The man with the bloody face was shouting and dancing up and down, but his voice was fainter. They swept around a curve, he was blotted out. There was nothing left of New Sparta but a confused, diminishing uproar and a dying redness in the sky.

He stopped splashing with his oar and put it down. The boat must be the little pleasure-boat which he and Sparta had used in their expeditions for turtle, Andrew noticed now. He wondered how seaworthy it would be when they got outside the bay.

Another thought struck him. Carlos, the boy, who was to have been with them.

"What happened to Carlos?" he said.

"At the last moment, he was afraid," said Caterina, calmly. "So he went with them."

"With who?"

"With the other Minorcans. They heard they were to be killed tonight, so they went away."

"Went away! In God's name, how could they go away?"

"The soldiers were busy. Mr. Cave had been to them and told them to revolt, but they did not trust him. So the old people met and decided. They told Mr. Cave they would be ready tonight, but as soon as it was night, they tied up their overseers and began to go away, one by one. A few were left, to deceive. The Italians did not stop them, they thought it was part of the plan. When they found out, it was too late. Mr. Cave had to choose between running after them and fighting Dr. Gentian."

Andrew gasped. So that explained Mr. Cave's grumbling. "Tricked, by God!"

If Dr. Gentian had been watchful or Mr. Cave loyal, so appallingly obvious a plan could never have succeeded—but the Doctor's watchfulness had been employed solely upon Andrew and Sebastian and Mr. Cave's treachery had wrecked his own scheme. Add to this the firm belief in the animal stupidity of the Minorcans which both Cave and his master held as a tenet of faith, and the thing was done. After years of rule, men grew careless, forgetting the ruled can have any craft. If Mr. Cave had won, he would doubtless have blamed the slaughter of Dr. Gentian on the departed Minorcans and, with Sparta's word to back him, could have looted the plantation as he pleased. Andrew pondered these circumstances in his mind.

"Did you know of this, Sebastian?" he said.

"When you told me what that dead man planned, I thought there must be some way out for my people. I told Caterina to tell them to do what seemed best and not think of us—that we would rescue ourselves."

The fact of Mr. Cave's death struck Andrew now with a queer force—he had hardly taken it in before. Mr. Cave would never dabble his fingers in Sparta Gentian's hair again or rave impotently

at the legitimate world. It seemed odd to think of
that strong, bulky body empty of violence—those
heavy hands no longer able to afflict or destroy.
There must be something left—a soul?—where was
it? He saw it fluttering in the wind like a burnt rag,
maimed, stupid, defiant and alone. "Poor devil,"
he thought for a moment—the rag fluttered at him
angrily—it did not want pity—it still wanted to
hurt but it no longer had the power—the thought
made him a little sick. . . .

"Think they'll chase us?" he said, after a while.

"Have their hands full," said Sebastian. "Cate-
rina says the Italians were going to pay off old
scores and fire the Greek huts. If they did, they'll
be fighting fire all the rest of the night."

They were far down the river now, the breeze
had freshened, the current ran smooth and fast. All
sound but the sound of water and wind and trees
had died away. Andrew trailed his hand over the
side and drew it up, dripping. His mind was quiet-
ing gradually. Already the furious scene in which,
such a short time ago, he had taken such active part
seemed unreal as a stage-play. Yet it had been real.
He had passed through just such a painted and
bedizened adventure as he had always envied and
wished against hope might be his own, when he was
a little boy playing under a table, listening to the
ship-captains and soldiers tell their sparse, enthrall-
ing tales. He had broken a prison—he had killed a

man—even now he was running away from death in a leaky pleasure-boat, perhaps to be wrecked on an island like Robinson Crusoe's, perhaps merely to drown. Yet it did not seem to him that this adventure was his, as the adventure in the tales had been his while he listened to them.

Now he knew why those tales had been so sparse and crudely-fashioned. When you were living a tale you did not have time to color it as it should be colored—your mind stuck on odd useless trifles—the teeth of a man you struck—the feel of an iron bar —the shape of a sail against the stars. Besides, in life, you were hungry and thirsty and had to make water—things which did not happen in a tale, or if they did, assumed heroic proportions. He felt betrayed, somehow, as he thought of this. Even he should have a trace at least of attractive venturesomeness upon him now, but if it were there, he could not see or feel it. The thought of the long, baking voyage still ahead of them brought no flavor of romance with it, no smell of strange flowers. It would be hot and irksome and dangerous, and he would be very glad when it was done.

Something splashed overside—Caterina was bailing the boat. He sighed and started to help her. After a while she stopped, but he went on.

"Tired, Caterina?" he said, in a pause.

"No—yes—but it does not matter," she said, with face half turned. She shut her eyes for an instant—

the moon laid a silver penny on each closed lid. He
stared at her face. Then she started to bail again,
and the slight charm was broken.

She gave a little sigh after a moment. "I think
they hit me, after all," she said in a commonplace
voice.

He crawled over to her, anguished suddenly.
"Where is it?" he said.

"There—ah"—his fingers touched something
sticky and warm. On her left side her dress was
soaked—blood or water?—he could not tell.

"Do you hear, Sebastian? She's hurt," he said,
in a sharp, angry voice. The dark figure at the tiller
moved uneasily, the boat shifted, spray blew in
Andrew's face.

"Is it deep, Caterina?"

"No, no—only a flesh wound—nothing—" But
her voice seemed changed. "See, when I put my
hand on it—it stops the blood."

Andrew put her hand aside, gently. He started
to tear a strip from his shirt to bandage the wound.
But the shirt was dirty and hard to tear. "Have
you a handkerchief—anything—Caterina?" he
asked anxiously. He felt in the darkness—she was
wearing a scarf at her waist. He held her up and
undid it.

"My poor scarf," she said, smiling. Her eyelids
fluttered and closed again—her face looked more
content.

He bandaged the wound as best he could with the scarf. "There, is that better?"

"Much," she said, and sighed lazily. "Thank you, *señor* Beard."

"Don't call me *señor*," said Andrew.

"I won't call you anything," she said, with a faint laugh. "I shall go to sleep. I am tired. Wake me when it is time to bail again."

He helped her to stretch out as comfortably as possible in the bottom of the boat, pillowing her head on the coat from which Sebastian had taken the button. Then he crawled back aft and crouched there, his head by Sebastian's knees. They were out in the little bay, now, the moonlight was ghostly on its white shelves of sand, the line of foam on the beach was a pale thread spun by a ghost on a shuttle of pearl. Presently they would run past the headland and the broad sea would take them.

Sebastian tested the wind. "Good," he muttered. "Can you handle her, amigo, after we get out of this bay?"

"Uh," said Andrew, nearly asleep. Sebastian laughed. "I'll wake you when you have to take her," he said.

Andrew threw back his head and looked up at the sky, breathing deep. The moon was a sailor's lamp now, a lamp of silver salt, sea-crusted, at the masthead of heaven. The stars were lights in a rigging. As he lay back he felt not only the movement of the boat, but a larger, vaguer roll, the roll of earth itself, a dark, huge ark plunging forward slowly through a black-and-silver waste. The slow way of that tremendous passage shook in his heart. He felt suddenly very happy and no longer dismayed by what might be in store for them. They had escaped, they were free. Caterina lay sleeping there in the bow: he could make out the huddle of her shoulder. In the morning he would see her as he had never seen her, familiar, friendly, with no mark of fear or oppression between her brows. They would live together always, somehow, Sebastian, Caterina and he—and gradually the stigmata of the stranger would depart from him and he would be able to read the runes enciphered in the ivory box of her heart.

His eyes, however, were closing. They could not really have closed, for it did not seem a moment before Sebastian nudged him to take the tiller and the sheet. Yet they stuck when he tried to open them, and when he had the tiller in his hand at last, the bay was gone and the boat was climbing endless hummocks of black-and-silver glass. It was rougher than it had been in the bay and the boat seemed diminished and apologetic in the wide face of ocean, but it settled to its work like a tired and patient pony, and after a few moments Andrew felt less afraid of drowning them all. The breeze was steady, he had little to do but follow the coastline and keep from going to sleep.

Twice he shipped unnecessary water and once just averted jibing disastrously in a sudden puff, then he settled back into the way of it as a man who has not ridden for some time settles back into the way of a horse. The heavy drowsiness of exhaustion no longer pawed at his throat—the black-and-silver monotony, the rushing of the near water, lulled him, but not toward sleep, rather into a shining, half-bodiless wakefulness. He felt that he could steer forever, through an endless, fluid universe of wet shadow streaked with radiance while the boat answered his hand.

2.

The sky was a flight of grey doves touched with faint, pink markings like the markings inside a seashell, the sea was a heap of rose-quartz and grey stones, the light that came seemed to struggle through dew and roughened glass. It was the illusory hour, the hour just before dawn, when the tide of the blood sets back toward life again, and birds ruffle their feathers, and a light wind rises from nowhere to run across the tops of grass-blades, shaking a crystal bauble, whose tiny clapperless bells utter only the ghost of sound.

Andrew, heavy-eyed, saw the boat and his companions solidify and emerge from a world where all was mist and water of light. Sebastian changed from a heap of sacks to a man asleep—there was a little fur of dew on his garments. Andrew looked down at his own shirt—yes, it too was damp and the tiller beyond his hand was beaded at the edges. Of a sudden he felt very cold and shivered. Well, he would be hot enough when the sun was up.

He stared at the shore-line, wondering how far they had come. He had no idea. Wet rocks and white beach—a palm-tree like a green feather duster on end—a hedge of wild Spanish bayonet on the brow of a cliff—it might be anywhere on the Florida coast. He felt lost and alone in a world, except for him and the sleepers in the boat, so completely deserted of humanity that he had the odd feeling he should breathe very slowly and gently or the whole misty picture of land and sea and sky would rise from around them in a sudden thunder of wings, like a flight of scared partridge, and leave boat and cargo swinging in a sparkling, measureless void. Now a gull rose squawking from between two humps of water and he took odd comfort in that harsh and living sound. The universe altered slowly from grey and rose as he watched the gull, the colors of morning deepened, the east caught fire from a burning bush.

The day would be hot and calm. Already the

wind was changing and dying as it changed. All day they would crawl over flawed sapphire under the point of a brazen arrow. He must wake the others. He wondered how much fresh water they had on board. He had crept in too near the coast— they were on the edge of rocky waters. Wake Sebastian, yes.

He leaned over and shook Sebastian by the shoulder. "Wake up!" he said. Sebastian stirred and groaned. Should he wake Caterina? He looked over at her where she lay in the bow.

Her head had slipped off his coat in the night; it was pillowed on her arm now, uncomfortably. Her other arm lay lax—the hand trailed in a puddle of water. He rubbed his eyes—she must be very tired to sleep in so cramped a posture. Then he saw that the red color in the puddle was not the reflection of the sun, and that, if she were sleeping, she slept with open eyes.

He was stumbling over to her, wildly, across Sebastian's body. The boat yawed violently and nearly flung him overboard. He heard Sebastian give a startled shout. Then he had her in his arms and the world was steady again.

"You're not dead," he kept saying to her. "You can't be dead." His hand passed over her forehead a dozen times, smoothing it. He felt at her wrist, at her heart, there was nothing to feel but flesh. Her fingers were cool, but it was the insensate coolness of wax and stone. The blood on her dress was drying already—she must have bled a great deal for all the water around her was stained.

Still holding her, he stared anxiously down at her face, trying to realize. This at least—death could not have come in horror but only as a slow dissolving tincture, for, though there was no smile upon them, her features were composed. She looked very tired and a little stern, but not dead as he thought of death. There was a stain on her mouth where she had bitten her lip: he wiped it off with his sleeve.

No, to her death could not have been as horrible as it might have been, but to him it was most horrible that she should have died so quietly, without a word. Perhaps she had meant to call out and had been too weak—he tried to remember dizzily if he had heard a sound in the night—she must have made some sort of sound. He could remember nothing.

He looked back. Sebastian was staring at them fixedly from the helm. His hand lay on the tiller as if he had forgotten it—a little muscle twitched in his cheek—his eyes were fey. Andrew thought, oddly, that he looked much as a man looks who has just got a sharp, excruciating blow in the groin—his mouth had the same sick stiffness.

He laid Caterina down. Then, bending over her, he looked ahead and felt a hoarse, startled cry tear out of his throat. "Rocks!" he yelled. "Sebastian! We're going on the rocks!" and fell in the stained water in the bottom of the boat as the boat jerked and the sail slatted over. There was a firm little jar beneath him like a sharp push from a heavy hand —a ripping sound—then catastrophe had passed, and they were going on again.

"Get out farther—from coast—" he said weakly, scrambling up. He looked back. Another moment and they would have struck that jagged line of black stumps full on. As it was they had just scraped across the edge where the water simmered uneasily like a bubbling pot. They had just escaped.

His feet were wetter than they had been. He stared down. A little spring of water was pumping up in the bottom, diluting the bloody puddles with fresh clear green. That slight firm push had been enough to ruin them. The boat was filling.

"Have to beach her, Sebas'," he said in a lifeless voice. "We're sinking."

Sebastian did not seem to hear: he was still staring ahead, with those blind, busy eyes, as if he were intent on counting every wave in the sea.

"Christ," said Andrew, flatly, and went back to shake him alive.

They beached the boat just in time. Twenty yards more to go or a rougher sea and they could not have done it. As it was, when a slow, huge roller took her at last and sludged her nose in the sand, she hesitated in its grip like a flogged, unwieldy mare, and the sea nearly took her and Caterina back again before they could haul up into safety. When they had done so, they lifted out Caterina's body between them and carried it up on the beach.

They had landed in a little cove. The sand was very clean and white—their footsteps dinted it sharply. It was morning now—the dew had vanished—the world was a glittering toy of silver and blue enamel.

"We must bury her," said Sebastian dully. "We cannot take her with us to consecrated ground." The muscle throbbed in his cheek. It was the first time he had spoken.

"I wish there were a priest," he said, looking about. "We must put up a cross." His mouth jerked.

Andrew followed his glance. There were other marks on the sand beside the marks of their footsteps and those of the gulls. A long slouching track crossed the beach and broke off at the edge of the rocks, the pawprints indented freshly like the marks of a devil's signet-ring.

"We can't just bury her and leave her," he said, with a shudder. He stared at the tracks. In the darkness something came down from the woods and pawed at a new mound.

He turned to his friend.

"Help me get some wood, Sebastian," he said, with a sob. "They can't hurt her if we burn her."

They toiled all morning, making the pyre. There

was driftwood scattered on the beach and, up a little gully, they came upon the dry, tindery carcass of a dead tree. At last, toward afternoon, they had enough and sat down to rest for a while and to try to eat. The hard bread and boucanned meat with which the boat had been provisioned was soaked and dirty, the water in the keg brackish and warm, but neither of them noted these things. Andrew heard the tinkle of running water, somewhere up in the woods. "Stream, Sebastian," he said, but he was too tired to go and look for it. He brushed the crumbs from his knees and rose. "Come along," he said.

The pyre was a tangled heap of wood—broken jackstraws cluttered together. They covered it with the sail, smoothing it out clumsily. Then they laid Caterina upon it. Sebastian had closed her eyes and her dress was as much in order as they could manage. Now Sebastian crossed her hands on her breast and, taking a little brass medal from a string about his neck, put it between them. "I should not have prayed for vengeance," he muttered, his mouth shaking. Then he got down.

They both stood for a moment, gazing. She lay reclined on the sail in a posture of stiff ease—she looked smaller than he remembered her, but neither pitiful nor strange. Andrew thought of the first time he had seen her, a barbarous saint, walking through the deep coils of night with a candle in her hand. She had seemed removed enough then, now she was forever removed. The fingers had been cool, the alien heart had carried a treasure secretly, wrapped in a gleaming cloth. Now the secret and she were air, he could follow them no longer, the treasure was lost, the runner in chains had shaken off the burden. What had been the mystery in the blood, so jealously guarded—the writing behind the eyes? Had she loved him, had she loved Sebastian, had she loved any man on earth? It did not matter now, she had taken her knowledge with her, clutched between stiff fingers, like a relic returned to its saint, secure alike from worshippers and blasphemers. It was gone, now, and with it had gone the youthful part of his heart.

He wished, idly, that he had not torn her scarf, the night before, to bandage her wound. She had not liked his tearing her scarf.

"Wait," he said, as Sebastian bent to strike the flint on the steel. He looked about desperately— there must be something else—something he could give. His glance fell on a bush of green spikes near the foot of the cliff. The Spanish bayonet was just coming into flower again, as he had seen it in flower, in Judge Willo's garden. He ran ploddingly over to the bush and thrust his hand among the thorns. His arm was bleeding from a dozen scratches when he pulled it out, but he had the flower. It had not yet come to full bloom, but it was enough.

He laid the white stalk on her breast—it rested there like an order bestowed by the Moon. He touched her fingers an instant. Then he crouched down at Sebastian's feet to blow the tinder into sparks.

The sparks hung for a moment and caught, the tinder started to burn. They fed the flame carefully, with small pieces, till it grew strong, then they stood aside. The bottom logs began to crackle, a little at first, then more. The driftwood burned eerily with ghosts of blues and greens, strange as the colors of an enchanter's rose; as it mounted, the flame grew purer.

Soon the whole pyre was well alight. The tiny cracklings blended into a fiercer, deeper utterance, strangely petulant in that quietude where the only other sound was the slow crash of a single, heavy breaker on the sand, repeated at even intervals like the firing of minute-guns for the burial of a mermaid queen in a tomb of coral and weed. Above the pyre the heat began to tremble in the still air like threads of isinglass. They could not have quenched the fire now if they had wished—it had become a furnace—the petulant mutter settled to a harsh, husky roar. Now the overlapping edge of the sail felt the pure aspiration of the flame—a wisp of smoke blew across Caterina's face—a running creeper of fire sprang up and crouched at her feet.

Andrew turned away. Sebastian was lying face down in the sand, his arms out, his body in the shape of a cross. He was silent, but now and then a convulsive shudder rippled the muscles of his back and broke.

Andrew looked blindly at the palm of his own hand, surprised to find it unscorched, undefaced by fire. He would not look at the pyre again, to see that body altered and the last revenge of flesh on spirit. So he looked once, hastily, but saw nothing but flame and smoke. Through the rest of his life, he thought, in stupor of mind, he would go his ways like a man caught up alive out of hell, with the rustle of fire always in his ears and the thin, acrid reek of it clung to his flesh.

They had to feed the fire once, when it slackened, but by then they were numb and went about the task like sleepers.

It was over at last. The pyre had sunk to a bed of ashes and sparks. There were charred things lying there, but they did not gather them up. What little wind there was had scattered some of the ashes, they could not tell which were hers. They heaped stones in a rough sort of cairn over the place and covered the stones with sand. Soon the mound looked as if it had always been there. At the top of the finished mound, Sebastian put a badly-fashioned cross—two pieces of wood lashed together with rope. Andrew looked at it, thinking the next gale would blow it down.

He had intended to cut a name on the cross, but the only knife they had was dull, and now there was no time.

He tried to recollect what he could of the burial service they read in Trinity Church, in the brown gloom, under the puffy busts of gilded angels. "I am the resurrection and the life," he muttered, but the remembered syrup of the minister's voice spoiled the words. Besides, any words seemed an affront to the bleak impermanence of that heap of sand and stones.

The sun was low in the sky—his shadow on the sand was long and black. They could not have mended the boat without tools and they had no tools but a musket and a dull knife. They would have to go on. They would have to try and find the road.

"We'd better get on," he murmured, lifting from the ground the little pack of bread and dried meat he had tied up in his coat.

3.

They had known before what it was to go on when they stood at the end of resource, now they were to know what it was to go on beyond that

end. There were two courses open to them—to
plunge into the woods at a venture, hoping to strike
the road and the Minorcans—or to attempt to reach
St. Augustine by the beaches, alone. They would
make better time at first, along the beach, but at the
end of the cove a headland jutted out into rocks
and they would have to swim for it. They chose
the woods, staking what was left them on finding
the road in the few hours of daylight 'that remained.

At first, it was easy. At the top of the gully they
climbed was a long open glade, full of lush, deep
grass. But at the end of the glade the underbrush
began. They tried to keep a straight course by
picking one tree out of the many to guide them, but,
as they had to fight their way through the under-
brush, their guidepost-tree would mix with other
trees, and though they would imagine they had
found the right one again, they could not be sure.
Their tree had had a lightning-blaze on its left side
—this one was blazed there too, but the blaze
seemed a different shape.

Twilight came and with it the fear of the woods,
the fear of going around and around the circle of a
tethered horse till at last something cracked in the
mind as they stumbled again upon the deep-trodden
track they had made before, and they began to strike
at the trees with their hands. The light faded in-
exorably, night crept between the trees, soft-footed,

dark-eyed. "Mustn't run," said Andrew to himself, plodding ahead through a confusion of shadows.

There was a dry stirring in the bushes at his right—a sound half-yawn, half-hiss, like the hiss of an angry cat. He froze. In his mind he could feel the blunt, cool, deadly head of a moccasin against his thigh. Indians, too,—he remembered the Indian he had seen peer out of a bush and vanish. "Musn't run," he repeated to himself with a gulp. It was very dark now. When he got back in a house, he would never let it be dark. He would sleep with a dozen candles flaring in his room and buy a slave to keep them tended all through the night. A bough stung his cheek. "Mustn't run," but, insensibly, he knew his pace had increased.

He plunged through a little thicket that seemed full of fish-hooks and came out upon an open space. Where was Sebastian? He couldn't hear Sebastian behind him any more. He stood trembling on the edge of the clearing like a beaten hound. He did not dare call to Sebastian—there might be no answer. If there were no answer, he would go quite mad.

"Mustn't run," he advised himself for the last time, and then, tearing the pack from his shoulders with a jerk, began to run blindly across the clearing on drunken feet, moaning to himself as he ran. Things struck at him with springy clubs, but he kept on, thrashing his arms against them like a drowning

man. Then at last the ground itself betrayed him
and gave way beneath him, and he was rolling into
a hidden pit where Fear and Night lay crouched
like twin spiders, ready to swathe him in suffocat-
ing, innumerable folds of glutinous, dark silk the
moment he touched bottom.

His next conscious memory was of a dark, con-
cerned face, grinning down at him through a red
shadow. *"Amigo,"* said the face, *"Amigo. Que tal,
señor?"* He grinned back at the face. It was
Carlos, the boy he had given a Spanish dollar, years
ago. He sat up, feeling his head spin. "Where's
Sebastian?" he said.

"Sebastian!" called the boy, joyously, "Sebas-
tian!" and now Sebastian came running out of the
red shadow with a wooden bowl in his hand. He
set the bowl down, and dropping beside Andrew,
kissed him solemnly and smackingly on both cheeks,
while Carlos clucked his approval. For a nervous
moment Andrew thought Carlos was going to kiss
him, too, but he did not. He trotted back toward
the campfire that made the red shadow, calling some-
thing as he went. Then Sebastian had picked up
the wooden bowl and was feeding Andrew hot, tasty
bits of pepper-stew with his fingers.

Their luck had turned at last. The Minorcans
had heard him shouting in the woods, and thinking
one of their stragglers had lost his way, had sent out
a party which came upon him as he rolled into the

road like a shot rabbit. He had missed Sebastian because Sebastian, a little behind him, had seen fire-light through the trees and had stopped to make sure. Then Sebastian had called to him, but his ears had been too full of his own terror to hear the call.

Revived by the stew, he listened eagerly to the news from New Sparta. A house-boy who had been unable to get away with the main body of the Minorcans had caught them up toward evening on a stolen horse. Of the post of eight soldiers, only the lugubrious corporal and a badly-wounded private remained. Dr. Gentian had been hurt in the fight but was alive, and Mrs. Gentian and the sub-overseers now ruled the wreck of the plantation. It was she who had checkmated Cave with a handful of her favorite Greeks—at the last moment there had been jealousy between the Greek and Italian sides of Cave's forces and the Greeks had finally decided to betray the revolt, just in time to save Dr. Gentian's life.

The Italians—what was left of them—were cowed. Some of them had managed to get hold of the sloop and take it half-way down the inlet, but there, having no sailors among them, they had stranded and decided to throw themselves on Mrs. Gentian's mercy. The colony was still unsettled and apprehensive, but Mrs. Gentian was definitely in the saddle and she rode with a tight rein. The

man did not know what policy she intended to
adopt towards the Minorcans—three messengers at
least had ridden for St. Augustine, but two of them
had already fallen into the Minorcans' hands, not
unwillingly—and she could not afford to send many
more.

Andrew asked for the other news, hesitatingly.
About Miss Gentian he did not know—she was
nursing her father, he thought. The words offered
Andrew an incredible picture. He saw Dr. Gentian
nightcapped, in a curtained bed, taking a cup from
Sparta with a weak hand. They were looking at
each other with blank, acquiescent eyes. That the
cup contained more than beverage seemed improb-
able. Both understood, both hated, but both were
under the whip, for the tall woman with the proud
nose and the secret mouth had come to her kingdom
at last and bound them equally, without compunc-
tion or passion. While she lived, they would live
as she willed, now. They had the strength of beauty
and violence and wit, but she had the strength of
silence, and her strength engulfed theirs, as the well
of darkness under the world engulfs its fallen stars.

He could see them living together for years—a
devoted family—a pair of serpents under an iron
bar, not daring to strike each other because the bar
was mute and cold, and they could not tell what it
would do if they struck. Some day Sparta, no
doubt, would marry—her mother's man, this time.

To the world they would present a united front. They would carry it off—oh, yes,—he trusted them for that.

He shuddered a little, seeing them all at table together, a year, five years from now. A curly-haired young man, dressed in the extreme of frippery, with a face as bland and foolish as a face painted on an egg, sat at Sparta's left, making table-talk to his new relations. Poor rabbit, thought Andrew, and smiled. The last shreds of youth's dearest delusion, the delusion that life will come to a climax of thunder and cease, fell from him silently. Only by accident was life as neat a workman as that. The climax might come a dozen times, but after each climax the workman would go on, like an idiot building a castle, adding story upon story to what was already complete.

His own life, by all canons of art and taste, should have finished when the last sand fell upon the mound on the beach they had left behind. Instead, here he was, eating pepper-stew, and relishing it, on the whole. If there were any moral inherent in the course of events which had happened to him, he had yet to descry it. But for accident he would be lying in the prison ditch with lead in his lungs, and Mr. Cave would be alive and roaring. Was he any better off as it was and Mr. Cave any worse?—he did not know. He felt that he was fast becoming a pagan and it hurt his sense of the fitness of things.

Then the Scotch strain in him, that drop which with the Jewish drop and the Irish, can survive a dozen admixtures of blood to dominate a mind, reasserted itself and told him grimly that it was not his business to question the schemes of God, but to hold on dourly to a predestined path between damnation and damnation, and distrust the vain speculations of the Egyptians. He could not quite believe its voice—would it call Caterina a vain Egyptian, he wondered—but it sufficed to send him off to sleep as soundly as if he were hearing John Knox preach.

4.

The camp broke up before dawn. The women gathered up their babies and their cooking pots—the head of the column straggled out in the road—the dust began to rise—the day's march was on. Andrew watched perhaps a quarter of the column pass, spectral in the early light, with a sense of dream, before he fell in the ranks at Sebastian's side. He had always liked the Minorcans, but his ruling impression of them had been one of gravity; he was amazed to see how lightly they seemed to take this wild expedition. They had left the promised land they had labored on for five years behind them and with it the greater part of their few possessions. They were marching to an unknown

futuie, perhaps to prison or death, but the general
mood seemed that of children ·on a holiday, and
ahead some boy was strumming a cracked guitar.

A child ran out of the ranks to pick a flower, was
brought back howling, and given a slap and a sweet-
meat. A mysterious Spanish joke on a plump young
man was passed from rank to rank with an accom-
paniment of laughter and pointing fingers. ¹Andrew
could see the back of the neck of the young man in
question, redden under its tan—then he turned to
fling back a snorting expletive over his shoulder and
the laughter grew ecstatic. One waddling matron
frankly sat down in the middle of the road to laugh
her fill and was promptly surrounded by a circle of
arguing, encouraging relations. A girl and a boy
had their hands locked together as they marched,
and the ranks around them turned into one vast
admiring family that tickled them with solemn or
ribald advice, to which they paid not the slightest
attention. A grave, white-bearded elder carried a
trussed live chicken under his arm—it squawked
incessantly and pecked at his sleeve.

They had few arms and scant provender—most
of the men had no better weapons than clubs or rude
wooden pikes. Sebastian was a person of great im-
portance since he carried a musket. An Indian
attack in force would mean massacre, a journey too
long drawn out the hunger pinch, but they seemed
to have considered these things and put them aside.

Now Andrew began to understand the quality in them that had taken them across an ocean to live in a strange land for five years under a rod without losing heart. There was a hardness hidden somewhere under their grace that called up all the Scot in him to answer it and he found himself whistling "The Bonny House of Airlie" as he trudged along in the dust.

5.

Grief, autumnal color of the stained and fugitive wood, sad vesture of red and gold, severe counsellor, true companion—your hands touch at the heart as lightly and idly as a child's and leave it shaken, then like a child you depart, on light feet, idly. Honest playfellow, candid guest, your company is strict, but for young men, brief; no matter how straitly the spirit would detain you, mind and body and time are too strong to endure for longer than a terse and appointed term so reticent a visitant. The earth stirs in its mail of frost, the geese begin to fly North again, the fire dies in the chimney, it is time for you to go. The wind will blow over the field but your voice will be in it no longer, the rain fall from the sky in showers, no longer austere with the echo of your sober bells. Now only the old, discarded traveller in the hearth-corner keeps your shadow alive in his breast, stretching out cold, knotted fingers before a diminishing flame.

That even the deepest sorrow can be transient was, however, 'a fact which Andrew, like most people, had to learn for himself. At first Caterina haunted the march for him, sleeping or waking, but even twenty-four hours made a little difference, not in the honesty of his grief but in its power to obliterate the rest of the universe. Certain things must be done, certain motions gone through. The constant activity of body, the uncertain immanence of danger, left no time for that luxurious melancholy which feeds upon a full stomach and an empty mind. Enforcedly, he began to live in the world again—the resurrection was painful and gradual enough but, once begun, it continued implacably.

6.

Four days later, the picture on the highway had changed somewhat in details but not in the whole. The same slow stream of humanity clotted the road, taking it easy to all appearances, yet stirring the dust relentlessly with passing feet. A child had died, 'another child had been born. The dead lay buried by the roadside, four men carried the new mother and her charge on an improvised litter toward the rear of the column. Tomorrow, or the next day, she would be back in the ranks again. The talk was less continual, faces showed fatigue,

feet went limping. But what talk there was seemed
cheerful, and those who fell behind for a while
straggled back into line eventually, some stronger
impulse than fear urging them on.

Andrew 'and Sebastian were at the head of the
column when they sighted the cavalry-patrol.

It was a small force, some twenty men in all,
commanded by a tall, leathery captain with a Lon-
don drawl, who kept blowing his nose on a lace
handkerchief because of the dust and then look-
ing around savagely at his men to try and catch a
smile on their faces. He commenced to shout at
the Minorcans in abominable Spanish when they
were yet some distance away, and though both
Sebastian and Andrew called back in English, it
seemed to make no impression on his mind for a
long·time.

"Damn my boots, what a precious lot of raga-
muffins!" Andrew could hear him saying to himself
as they approached. "You can't talk their lingo,
can you sergeant? I thought not—a pretty affair,
damn my boots, to send a gentleman with his Maj-
esty's commission to shepherd a pack of mutinous
blackguards into town. If the governor were of my
mind, he'd shoot down every last man jack of them
in the ditch of the fort, by pox and thunder—don't
you think so, sergeant? Hey, you there, the man
with the dirty shirt—" he called suddenly as
Andrew came nearer, "can you talk English?

Damn my boots he's staring at me like a codfish—
why don't you salute an officer, man? Stap me,
the creature stinks in the wind like Billingsgate fish-
market! Talk English, fellow! Parlay English,
Anglish—yes—no?" he howled abruptly at Andrew
from a distance of five paces, as if Andrew, being a
foreigner, must be stone-deaf.

It did not surprise Andrew to be taken for one of
the Minorcans. Wth a ten day's beard on his face
and his skin burned by the sun, he could have passed
for a scavenger. He was only surprised when the
captain, after a few interchanges, grew fairly civil
on the whole. He was like other English officers
Andrew had known, apparently in a continual sweat
of puzzled exasperation whenever he had a task to
accomplish, and yet somehow getting the task done
with a certain slack efficiency that seemed to sur-
prise himself. His bloodthirstiness was entirely a
matter of conversation. Andrew saw him later in
the day with a fat Minorcan two-year-old on the
saddle before him and an expression of weary fury
on his face, muttering savagely, "Damn my boots,
you think you're a fine whelp, don't you—a fine
little piece of mutiny to boil for officers' soup—
how he claws at me, damme sergeant! I think I'd
better drop him in the road and break his head."
But his arm was tightly clutched around the child,
and the child was squeaking delightedly as it pulled
at the horse's mane.

Andrew made himself as inconspicuous as possible during the rest of the march and did not attempt to interview the captain till it was ended. A year ago he would have done so at once, without thinking how strange his important talk of the house of Alexander Beard and Son would sound on the lips of a dirty, unshaven boy. Now he knew his cue was self-effacement till he could get to the Governor. From the talk of the patrol he gathered that His Excellency was at least not ill-disposed toward the Minorcans and intended to give them a chance to state their case. But he and Sebastian stood in a different position from the rest of the host.

The other Minorcans could come into court with hands clean of anything but a bloodless rebellion against an unjust employer. Sebastian and he had been charged with murder and treason—Sebastian had killed Mr. Cave—both had broken prison—to mix their grievance with the general one would only impair the latter's chance of redress. On the other hand, if the Governor were really Dr. Gentian's foe, Andrew's testimony, being that of an Englishman, might clinch the matter definitely in the Minorcans' favor. He had plenty of time to think the matter through from every angle, and decided finally, that his best course was to keep his identity hidden till the end of the march came.

7.

They were camped on the outskirts of St. Augustine at last. The captain had held a long interview with the prominent men of the colony. In the afternoon, the Governor would ride out to see them. Meanwhile, they must be patient. A small ration-party might go into town, but the main body was to remain in camp and fraternize as little as possible with the townspeople. He gave his word for the safe-conduct of the ration-party and his assurance that if these conditions were fulfilled, the Governor would grant them a fair and open hearing.

Then he solemnly posted sentries between the camp and the town. It was purely for effect—both he and the Minorcans knew that if the five hundred wished they could brush aside the sentries and descend on the town like locusts. But, being for effect, it served. Hemmed in by a larger force, the Minorcans would have begun to mill like frightened cattle. As it was they settled down quietly enough, the women to tending their children, the men to listen to the boy with the cracked guitar or to try and repair gear damaged on the road.

Now, thought Andrew, the time had come for him to make his stroke. He asked to speak with the captain in private and in a few words stated his name and his wish for an interview with the Governor.

"Damn my boots and breeches," said the captain,

staring at him keenly, while his hand drummed on the pommel of his saddle, "I thought you spoke odd English for a Spaniard—but, body of hell, what a tale! I wouldn't have believed—to be frank, sir, even for a gentleman in straits, you make a damned queer appearance, if you'll excuse the remark."

"My grandfather carried a pack," said Andrew, deliberately, smiling. The dream of the Beards of Westmoreland departed forever as he said it, leaving no scar behind. He might play the exquisite again, when he had money and clean clothes, but never without a certain feeling of masquerade. In theory, one could always tell a gentleman, no matter how dirty he was—in practice, the matter seemed a trifle more complicated.

"Oh, well—" said the captain, apparently somewhat relieved. He stared at Andrew again. "It sounds so damnable odd," he confessed frankly, "Of course you'll have some acquaintance in the city to—." He waved his hand.

Andrew thought. He could hardly call on any of the gentlemen he had met at Judge Willo's to bear out his story—they were all Dr. Gentian's intimates.

"The Governor might remember me, if I were shaved," he said slowly, "and then—is the Pride of the Colonies still in port? Captain Stout would recognize me, I know."

"Oh, if that's your man!" said the captain, "Cap-

tain Stout's with the Governor now, I imagine—
he's had the devil of a time getting cargo—and then
the Governor's been holding him back to question
him about this insurrection in the North. He
sails this afternoon—you may catch him at the Gov-
ernor's if you make haste. Sergeant—Sergeant—"
he called peevishly, "where's one of those damned
horses? I want to mount this man and send him to
the Governor."

He turned sharply to Andrew. "You'll watch
yourself in the town," he said. "They're going to
burn some of your rebels in effigy in the square
today—silly nuisance burning fellows in effigy, but
looks damned well as an expression of loyalty in a
report"—and he laughed like a fox barking.

"Sergeant—take this man into town with you and
see he gets to His Excellency."

"Shall I tie him, sir?" said the sergeant, stolidly,
saluting.

"Damn your boots, no. Why are you such a
damned old fool? You can knock him on the head
if he tries any tricks," he added thoughtfully, "but
don't tie him now."

8.

So Andrew, for the second time, presented to the
streets of St. Augustine a queer and disreputable
figure, under the hot sun. But this time, though he

was ragamuffin indeed, he cared not at all where at first he had cared so greatly. He scuffed his broken shoes in his stirrups, comfortably, and was only interested to note that a little tail of pointing, giggling children followed himself and the sergeant to the Governor's door.

"He see the Governor!" said a dewlapped Paunch with an amber-topped cane, regarding Andrew with evident disgust. "He can't see the Governor! Ridiculous, sergeant! The Governor's closeted—even if he were not—the fellow's far too foul."

"Captain Strahan's orders. To see His Excellency at once," repeated the sergeant metallically. Andrew gathered that he did not like the Paunch.

"Captain Strahan's orders?" yammered the Paunch, nervously. "Well, why didn't you say it was Captain Strahan's orders—if you'd said it was Captain Strahan's—"

The Paunch's importance had shrunk—he was bustling away through a door.

"Silly old capon," said the sergeant, devastatingly, with the air of one who spits to relieve his mind.

The Paunch was back again, ushering Andrew along with fat, fluttering hands. The sergeant clanked after them.

"No tricks," he was muttering. "Captain's orders. No tricks at all."

Then a door was flung open and Andrew stumbled into a big, cool room where two men were facing each other across a desk. Both looked up as he entered. The next moment a chair went to the floor with a crash—and the hard paws of Captain Stout were gripping both his hands.

It was later. Andrew and the Governor were alone. He had told his story in detail, with certain suppressions, chiefly involving Sparta and the killing of Mr. Cave. The Governor had put a number of questions, most of them in regard to things that seemed to Andrew of little importance. Now at last he seemed satisfied.

Andrew had tried to gage him during the interview. He was a narrow man and a touchy one, but he seemed honest. Of his long-banked hate of Dr. Gentian there could be no doubt whatever—it showed in every line of his face when the name came up. Andrew's description of the conditions at New Sparta had seemed to shock him genuinely, though not quite in the way that Andrew had expected. He seemed much more shocked, for instance, at Dr. Gentian's failure to inform him fully that he had arrested Andrew as a traitor.

"It won't do," he kept saying. "Won't do; man must be mad. Political prisoners should be brought before me at once."

"Well, sir!" said Andrew finally, when there seemed to be no more questions the Governor wished to ask.

The Governor fiddled with his inkstand a moment. Then he looked at Andrew.

"You've put me in a queer position, Mr. Beard," he said at length. "Oh, I don't doubt your story. It only confirms what I've suspected, ever since the colony started—but my predecessor was a firm friend of Dr. Gentian's and—". He frowned. "Damn it, if I could only put you in the witness-box," he burst out. "As it is, I half-wish you'd never come to see me at all."

"I'm sorry," said Andrew. It seemed the only possible remark.

"Oh, don't apologize," said the Governor, worriedly. "After all you've done me a service. My mind's made up now. Oh, I've no doubt the Minorcans would have proved their point in any case, but your tale clinches it for me. They shall have their rights, Mr. Beard. I'll settle them here—God knows a couple of hundred good workers will be a godsend to the town. But now, Mr. Beard." He rapped on the desk. "What are we going to do with you?"

"I am quite at your disposal sir," said Andrew, drawing a vast breath of relief.

"No, no," said the Governor, querulously, "that's just what you can't be. If you stay here, some of Gentian's friends are sure to stir up trouble about that absurd charge of treason he's brought against you." He smiled. "Officially, Mr. Beard, I have not as yet, as I say, been informed of that charge through the proper channels. But if someone here should take it into his head to lodge a direct accusation—I should have to notice it—yes—I should have to notice it—I should have to hold you for examination, Mr. Beard—and then, damn it, the moment I do"—he exploded again, "the fat's in the fire and the whole Minorcan case is muddled with yours."

"Of course, sir, if you wish to"—began Andrew, slowly.

"Examine you? In God's name, why?" said the Governor, brusquely. "I know your father's name— Captain Stout's told me of the sacrifices he's already made for the Crown." Captain Stout had obviously omitted any mention of Lucius, and Andrew was very grateful. "If you were a traitor, why the devil would you be sitting here talking to me?" the Governor ended. The question seemed unanswerable, and Andrew himself began to wonder why.

"No, Mr. Beard," the Governor went on. "The charge against you is absurd, but it must not be pressed. I've no doubt Captain Stout will trust your father's son for a passage to New York. When you reach there, you will, naturally, join the army. They say De Lancey's raising a troop of loyalist horse—well, Mr. Beard, there's my advice, unofficially. Do you find it reasonable?"

"Most reasonable, your Excellency," said Andrew, with a slight smile. "I shall, as you say, return to New York at once—and join the army."

"Good," said the Governor, rising. "I shan't ask you for a deposition, Mr. Beard—it will be best if your name is not brought in at all. You'll find Captain Stout in the anteroom—and I should advise you going aboard at once, if I may suggest it."

"I have to say goodbye to a friend," said Andrew. "After that I shall go aboard as soon as possible."

"A friend?" said the Governor. "Oh, yes—the Minorcan boy who was in prison with you. I wish we could get him away too. He'll only serve to confuse things—and I want a clear case." He looked at Andrew.

"Perhaps it can be managed," said Andrew, thanking his gods for the narrow strength of the Governor's hate of Dr. Gentian, that now blinded him to everything but the prospect of the latter's ruin. "Good day, your Excellency—and thank you."

"Good day, Mr. Beard, and a safe voyage," said the Governor, turning back to his papers, and Andrew bowed and retreated from the lion's jaws.

9.

He had arranged to meet Sebastian in the Plaza, near noon, if Sebastian could get leave from the ration party—and it was there he now proceeded with Captain Stout. The matter of his passage was

settled—Captain Stout had offered it, before he had
had time to speak. He mentioned Sebastian. "Body
servant, too, I'm sure," said Captain Stout, ami-
cably, and Andrew thought it best not to explain
further at present. He looked at Captain Stout as
they walked along, trying to read his political opin-
ions in his face, but he could make nothing out of
those weathered features.

Fooling the Governor or letting him fool himself
was one thing; he did not like the idea of fooling
Captain Stout. But then, even yet—was he quite
sure of his own intent? He had been quite sure;
but in the Governor's room, with its air of power
and order long established, the old colors of things
had crept back to them insensibly, making a world
where rebels were rebels and no gentleman in his
wits thought of fighting for anything but a king.
He sighed, cursing himself 'for a vacillation he could
not help—habit and custom are strong chains. But
he was a shopkeeper's son, not a gentleman in his
wits . . . oh, well, look at the people in the streets
and put off thinking for a while. The narrow
streets were crowded with people going to the Plaza;
when they came to the Plaza, it was crowded too.

"Is this a fiesta day?" he asked of his companion.

"Not exactly," said the captain, slowly. "They
ware talking about burning some Guy Fawkses or
something—I'm as glad my boys are on board
except for the boat's crew—"

Then Andrew remembered. The demonstration
of loyalty. He saw a pile of 'wood in the center of
the square and was horribly reminded of another
such pile of wood he had helped to build. His heart
began to pound. He wanted to get away. 'But
Sebastian must be found first—ah, there he was,
standing in the mouth of an alleyway. Andrew
threw up his hand and called out over the sea 'of
heads. Sebastian heard him, turned, waved back,
and started to worm his way toward them, as a
ragged shout went up from the other side of the
square.

A drum was beating, a voice was calling, "Make
way! Make way!" The crowd chattered and jos-
tled. From the cramped mouth of the street on the
other side of the square a procession debouched, the
crowd fell away before it. Andrew felt Captain
Stout's grip tighten on his arm. Now the head of
the procession was out in the square itself—a rout
of men dressed in sorry rags of carnival. Some had
faces blacked with soot, like boys on Guy Fawkes'
Day, others wore painted ludicrous masks. They
were singing and shouting—the crowd roared its
approval—the front ranks pressed back on the toes
of those behind to leave a clear path to the woodpile
in the center.

Then Andrew heard himself saying, "Damn you!
Damn you all!" in a hurried whisper, as the effigies
came into sight. There were two of them, great

lolling dummies of straw, absurdly garbed, borne high on the shoulders of the crowd. They had halters around their necks, before them marched a man with a butcherlike face, dressed in hangman's black. A rope was slung over his arm and he carried a placard on a pole—"Death to all traitors!" in Spanish and English. There were other placards in the crowd, and two signs flapped at the bellies of the dummies. Andrew could make them out now, "Jackie Hancock"—"Sammy Adams"—

A gratified whoop went up from the crowd at the sight of the dummies. A big, sweating woman with a large pink chamberpot in her hand skipped nimbly out of the crowd and flung the contents of the vessel in the face of the dummy marked "Adams," with a shrill, joyous scream, splattering its bearers.

Andrew wrenched himself loose from Captain Stout's hand. "Stop it—stop it—you Spanish bastards—" he was crying, with tears of rage in his eyes. He saw a thousand grinning faces turned toward him, and struck at the nearest wildly, fighting and going down.

10.

A young man with a newly-broken head lay in a tossing bunk in the cabin of a ship at sea, and began to feel the first qualms of seasickness taint his relative content. He stirred, and said as much.

"Means you've come out of it nicely," said Captain Stout, bending over him. "You'll be pleased to know, Mr. Beard—the man that hit you with the stick'll carry a thick ear some time yet," he added.

"I acted like a fool," said Andrew. "I don't see how you got away. But I couldn't stand the woman."

"There," said the Captain, soothingly. "It's natteral. Young blood's hot. *I* wasn't too pleased," he went on. "No, we wasn't any of us too pleased with the goings on. Told 'em you were one of my crew with a touch of sun. They swallowed it. I wanted to tell them something else. But you'll thank your Spanish friend—I couldn't have got you off alone—let alone talk their jabber fast enough—"

"What happened to him?" said Andrew feebly.

"He's here." The Captain chuckled. "Ain't you, Spanish?"

"*Si señor*," came a voice from the upper bunk. "But sick as a soldier. How are you, my friend?"

"Much as you are," said Andrew, and laughed. "I'm glad you're here, Sebastian."

"*Gracias*," said the voice from above. "We changed knives—I follow my knife. Besides," he added, after a moment, "I, too, have a certain desire to help the donkey we spoke of kick off his rider. The rider wears too red a coat to suit me."

"What about you, Captain?" said Andrew, after a pause.

"Oh, we're all liberty-boys, now," said the Captain, with a casual chuckle. "Didn't say so before, you being your father's son; but we're all liberty-boys on the Pride now—if I didn't tell the Governor. Lord, I thought he'd have me a dozen times, but I never saw a soldier that wasn't a turniphead."

"Does my father know you're a liberty-boy, sir?" said Andrew, smiling.

"Not yet," said the Captain. "That'll go hard, it will. Well, I thought I'd do my duty by him, this last time. And then, if it's going to be as long a war as I reckon it, what's the harm in doing a bit of trading first?" He spat out the porthole. "Seem queer at the start, going counter to old King George," he added thoughtfully. "Not that I've ever seen the man, but I've always had a sort of picture of him. Well, life's unexpected and that's a fact." He seemed to take comfort in the truism.

"They've got a flag with a rattlesnake on it," he continued. "Liberty or Death. It'll be queer to raise it. The Pride's had British colors up ever since she was launched. She's used to them. Well, she'll have to learn new ways. I hope she'll like them, but I'm doubtful." He shook his head.

"We'll all have to get used to new ways," said Andrew. He stared into the future, trying to pierce it, but he could see nothing. It did not matter, his own course was plain.

"How long will it take us, Captain?" he said.

"Couldn't say, Mr. Beard, but the rumpus'll still be going when we get back. The lobsters think it won't, but it will. You see, King George Third's gone too far—and we mean to break loose now. That makes the difference."

"I suppose so," said Andrew, lying back and thinking of all that had passed since he last lay in a ship's bunk. What had he got from all of it— what had he done? The Minorcans had rescued themselves—he had not even killed Mr. Cave. Caterina—he had not thought much of that mound in the little cove since they had left it, he had not had time or strength. He thought of it now. She had saved him, her he had been unable to save. He had only been able to leave a part of his youth where she lay, for the wind to blow off like ash. Even now he was not sure that he had loved her, as he understood love—nor could he see her his, in life, by any fantasy of mind. There had been a spell between them—an incantation—it had worked itself out and passed—gone back beyond the moon. For the last time, as the ship tossed and the sea grew rougher, the shape of the Spanish bayonet arose in his mind, with its thorns and its white flower, incongruous, enchanted, pure.

Out of all the confused and brilliant turmoil of the past year that visionary semblance alone remained steadfast—that semblance and his friend Sebastian—perhaps they were enough.

Yet he trembled, hurt and aching, uncomforted by the knowledge that hurt and ache would pass, as in time they would, and become only a colored memory, a ghost of perfume. Now he only knew that he wanted to hear Caterina's voice, and that she was dead. But even at the worst of this bitterness, other thoughts came—New York—Lucius—a musket—a rebel army—a lion and a unicorn hunted through green Massachusetts woods. In a short while, unconsciously, he found himself seeing Sebastian and a boy with his own face cooking hominy on a griddle over a soldier's campfire. His inexperience of war lent the picture a plausibility, a charm almost. The risen sun cast a broad path of illusion at the feet of the two figures, the blue smoke of the fire fluttered, there was a smell of burning leaves in the air. Soon enough the drum would assert its sharp, monotonous scorn.

"Well, sir," said the Captain, "you'll be feeling better tomorrow." He was going now. "No objection to your Spanish friend bunking in with you?"

"No. He's my friend," said Andrew, as if in explanation of more than the question had asked. "Good night, Captain."

"Good night, Mr. Beard. You'll find dirty weather when you get up tomorrow—it's coming on to blow."

THE END